INTRODUCTION

The twenty-third of December 2023. It is 2 a.m. in Yamoussoukro, the capital of Ivory Coast. I have just been elected president of the second-oldest political party in Africa, the PDCI-RDA, with support from 96.5 per cent of the 4,000 delegates attending the party's congress.

The speech-making is over. I've spent hours thanking my supporters individually, shaking hands and posing for selfies. In the enormous conference hall of the Foundation Houphouët-Boigny, workers are tidying up. The last of the party members – conversations and celebratory drinks finished – are climbing into buses and heading to their hotels.

I sit in the front row of the cavernous room, feeling stunned by the significance of what I have just achieved, after a tough campaign. I reflect on the strange circularity of my journey, the echoes of the past growing louder the longer I rest, upright in an orange chair. Yamoussoukro is named after a direct ancestor, Yamousso. Kro means town, so this is literally Yamousso's town. This is our family's home town.

The Democratic Party of Ivory Coast – African Democratic Rally (PDCI-RDA) was founded in 1946 by Félix Houphouët-Boigny, my great-uncle, independence leader and the first President of Ivory Coast. He is buried nearby, as are my great-grandmother, my grandmother, and my mother. My father was jailed a few miles away.

I had been to pray at Houphouët-Boigny's tomb earlier in the day, to pay my respects. I murmured to him that I was running for his job and asked for his blessing. A deep sense of gratitude coursed through me as I remembered the scene. 'Thanks,' I thought, a smile breaking out spontaneously on my lips.

Just a week before, this moment of triumph looked as if it might elude me. We had initially organised the congress in the commercial capital, Abidjan, booking the city's biggest hotel for delegates. The catering and transport had been paid for in advance. Around 6,000–7,000 people were expected. But on the eve of the event, as party members arrived from all corners of the country, a judge issued an order suspending the party meeting.

At a hearing without our lawyers present, a judge heard complaints from two party members (out of 6,800 delegates) who said they had been illegally excluded from the ballot. When we asked why we were not called as witnesses, court officials said they were unable to contact the party. This would be like a court in Washington DC suspending the Democratic Party convention and claiming it was impossible to contact a Democrat party official.

I learned about the decision at around two in the morning. A sympathetic senior police officer called my sister to tell her that the police had received an order to prevent the congress by 'whatever means necessary'. That meant possibly using live ammunition.

Soon afterwards, party delegates began ringing me. A large police force, travelling in around forty buses, had arrived and were confiscating sound equipment, banners and party merchandise.

Several things were immediately clear to me: the congress would not take place, and this was a provocation. The court decision was intended to create disorder.

When you've spent a lifetime observing African politics, you're prepared for these moments. Under Alassane Ouattara, President of Ivory Coast since 2011, the country has slid progressively into authoritarianism. In such regimes, leaders do not crudely arrest or

Without Prejudice

TIDJANE THIAM

Without Prejudice

A Memoir

Breaking Barriers, Building Bridges –
from City Boardrooms to the Ivory Coast

WILLIAM
COLLINS

William Collins
An imprint of HarperCollins*Publishers*
1 London Bridge Street
London SE1 9GF

WilliamCollinsBooks.com

HarperCollins*Publishers*
Macken House, 39/40 Mayor Street Upper
Dublin 1, D01 C9W8

First published in Great Britain in 2025 by William Collins

1

A catalogue record for this book is
available from the British Library

ISBN 978-0-00-871878-7 (Hardback)
ISBN 978-0-00-871879-4 (Trade paperback)

Set in Adobe Caslon Pro
Printed and bound in the UK using 100%
renewable electricity at CPI Group (UK) Ltd

To my mother, with love.

CONTENTS

imprison their political opponents; they maintain a surfeit of democratic legitimacy. They use the court system and push their opponents deliberately outside the law.

After the suspension order, I spent the night defining our strategy, prevailing over other party figures who preferred confrontation, through a righteous and justifiable sense of anger. I maintained that we had to respect the court decision and prevent violence at all costs. 'You cannot go outside the law. We'll all get arrested, and no one will defend us,' I argued.

My statement to supporters and delegates at 8 a.m. made this explicit. I urged them to leave the hotel where the meeting had been due to take place and await further instructions from the party.

Later in the day, the provocations increased. With thousands of delegates milling around in Abidjan with no congress to attend, police went to occupy our party headquarters. A standoff ensued, with hundreds of members seeking to protect the building and police massing outside. I decided to go there in person.

Standing on the side of my SUV to address the crowd, with lines of armed police a few metres from me, I urged everyone to demonstrate the best of our party. 'We are not going to go down to this level,' I said. 'We are going to show everyone that we are a party of peace and a party of the rule of law.

'In life you never control events, but you can always control how you react to them,' I continued. 'We will not answer this provocation and fall into the trap set for us.'

I promised that our congress would be reorganised, that a vote would take place, and I would be a candidate. They would be able to elect me if they so wished.

The day ended with the architects of chaos disappointed. The evening news did not have images of street fires, tear gas and protestors throwing stones. No bodies lay crumpled in the streets. Hundreds of police reinforcements boarded their buses again and went home. I felt like I had won the moment, inflicting a defeat of sorts on the regime.

I knew it was only a first skirmish along what would be a long and treacherous road to the presidential elections in October 2025. There would be other confrontations, more dirty tricks.

We eventually managed to track down the two delegates who had filed the legal cases which had been used as justification to suspend the congress. Both were in hiding. They were low-level party officials. Both were clearly being used, bribed and manipulated. We managed to persuade them to withdraw their cases. They would have to reappear in court in any case and the flimsy basis of their appeals could be easily demonstrated.

A week later, we reconvened in Yamoussoukro. After the voting, the results were read out district by district, region by region. Our strategy of reaching out to members individually, a hugely time-consuming and resource-intensive operation, had been extremely successful. In many places, I had 100 per cent of the vote.

I became only the third president of the party in its seventy-seven-year history, the first being Houphouët-Boigny. It was another major swing in fortune.

Who would have thought that almost four years after one of the most dramatic moments of my life, I would be in a position to become the next president of my country. What a contrast to 7 February 2020.

That fateful day was my last as CEO of Credit Suisse, the second-largest bank in Switzerland at the time, and one of the most important financial institutions in the world. I left in extraordinary circumstances, having completed a three-year restructuring that moved the bank from having the weakest capital position of twenty-seven European banks to stronger foundations. I had carried out all the hard, disruptive, thankless work: the cutting and streamlining, the closing and reorienting. I had returned the bank to profitability in the process: 2019 was its best year in a decade. And yet I was leaving after years of vicious and relentless attacks by rabid sections of the German-speaking Swiss press and portions of the Zürich establishment.

If my experiences have taught me anything, it is that we are constantly vulnerable to unexpected twists in the plot we attempt to write for ourselves, the leftfield events that mess up the best-laid plans. One of the most important personal qualities you can possess is an ability to react and rebound. Taking a long-term perspective, learning from adversity, and maintaining a good sense of humour, all help build the sort of resilience that is important in life – and African politics.

As my dear departed father used to say with a chuckle: 'The most important thing in life is not to die.' It was said to remind us about the gift of life, and was typical of his humble outlook, informed by a lifetime spent far closer to the snapping jaws of mortality than most people experience today in wealthy developed countries.

So when our party congress was blocked, I didn't overreact. When my time at Credit Suisse came to an end, I didn't feel that my world had collapsed. I didn't feel embarrassed or ashamed. I recognised it as just another curveball in a journey that has contained several, including a 1999 coup in Ivory Coast that led me to leave the country for two decades, or the Covid pandemic, which saw me take on a role coordinating economic help for the African continent.

Documenting such moments and writing about my life became one of a multitude of new projects, both personal and professional, that have emerged in the last few years. My hope is that they might inform and help others who identify with my story – or not.

It's a journey that will take us from my homeland to North Africa, to France, the United States, to Asia, and on to the boardrooms of two of Europe's biggest financial institutions in London and Zürich. It's a story about Africa, about Europe, about Asia, about emigration; about the rewards of hard work, the stupidity of racism, and the value of our capitalist model. It also contains many of my thoughts, informed by three decades in the public and private sectors, on how politicians and business people might help fight poverty, encourage development and promote human dignity – the focus of my time and efforts now.

It begins in Abidjan, my birthplace, the birthplace of my children, and the anchor point for my identity that has come to incorporate multiple influences over the past sixty-two years.

Chapter 1

Early Challenges

For the first years of my life, I was a boy without a father. It wasn't that I didn't have one; he just wasn't there. He existed in the photographs placed around our home, a whitewashed colonial-era mansion in Abidjan. There were pictures of him all over the house, smiling with my mother, often dressed in a suit and tie, shaking hands with important-looking people.

He existed too in the memories and stories of my older siblings, six of them in total. The eldest, my brothers Daouda and Boubacar, were far more affected by his absence than I was, the pup of the family, too young to remember the day he was taken away. My elder siblings felt not just the emotional void caused by his disappearance, but the pall of uncertainty and disgrace it cast across our family.

My father existed too in the words of my mother. Once I was old enough to understand, as a headstrong toddler, she would seek to reassure me. 'You have a father. But he's in prison,' she'd say while pointing at his picture. 'He'll be home one day.' She believed it too. Convinced of his innocence, she was working her formidable network of contacts to free him, with single-minded devotion.

But truth be told – as my consciousness expanded to take in the world around me for the first time – my father's absence was no stranger to me than the other extraordinary circumstances of my early life: the buzz of servants around the house, built on the so-called Plateau of Abidjan, prized for its breeze and fresh air; the hum of air conditioning that kept the house miraculously cool while others sweated outside in the city's thick humidity; my mother's shiny black Fiat that turned heads when we glided by to the market. Only much later, with the benefits of education and travel, was I able to make sense of any of this.

My father missed my first words, as well as my first trip around our palm-fringed garden on my bike, a red tricycle. In 1963, the year after my birth, he had been accused of conspiring against the president, Félix Houphouët-Boigny – my mother's uncle. Having reached the highest point of his career, serving as information minister at the time, and the peak of his social ascension, he crashed to earth in spectacular fashion.

He had been rounded up by police in September 1963 during a cabinet meeting at the presidential palace. As he and other ministers had taken their places at the large oval table, the doors opened, and police swept in. Names were read out to the dazed, seated figures. Those identified were informed that they were being taken into custody.

Scared but resigned to their fate, my father Amadou and around a dozen others were led away to cells in the basement of the palace. My mother learned the news on the country's unique television channel that my father had so proudly helped launch just a few weeks earlier on Independence Day 1963 – Ivory Coast becoming the first former French colony to have its own television service.

The detentions were part of a round of arrests ordered by Houphouët-Boigny, who had become convinced – through the devious scheming of those around him – that some of his ministers were plotting against him. A first purge in 1962 had not been enough. This second time, even men like my father, who had served Houphouët-Boigny loyally during the fight for Ivorian independence, were rounded up.

After several months of detention without visits, the alleged plotters were taken to a prison that Houphouët had built especially in Assabou, near Yamoussoukro, his and our ancestral village. He felt he could only trust guards from his tribe with such important prisoners. The jail was nicknamed 'the college' by detainees – gallows humour, as they thought Houphouët wanted them to learn a lesson in loyalty.

The prison was later bulldozed as everybody, jailed and jailers, looked to move beyond this episode in the country's history.

Detention conditions had been tough there, and a life was lost. Ernest Boka, a renowned jurist and former president of the Supreme Court, died at Assabou prison a few days after being arrested in April 1964. According to the official version, Boka hanged himself after leaving a suicide note. Some of the inmates always maintained he had been killed during one of many violent interrogations.

Detainees were frequently beaten until they volunteered names of other supposed traitors, who would in turn be arrested and beaten. One saving grace was that the detainees were held in a large cell with their peers, fellow independence activists, many of whom, like my father, had experienced colonial repression and jail during the struggle for independence from 1946 to 1960. What might have broken other men appeared to my father like a test, to be overcome, another challenge in a life of obstacles. He would later tell me how some of his contemporaries, grown used to a life of abundance outside, would beg to be given whisky or other comforts. He didn't suffer from the privations, he told me.

The notion of resilience has become a contemporary buzzword, explored endlessly in books, newspaper articles and social media posts. Why do some people seem to have it and others not? How do you develop it? Where does it come from? Perhaps a lucky few have innate reserves, but it appears to me to be something like mental muscle, built up over a lifetime of exercise. It explains why many people who grow up poor in developing countries, exposed to the vagaries of life without the buffer of money or a modern state, often possess it in spades.

This knowledge has always given me a sense of proportion in my own career. The challenges I would later encounter in the City of London or in Zürich, would seem trivial next to the injustice of being imprisoned for a crime you did not commit, or the daily struggle for survival that my father had once endured – and which so many of my compatriots face today.

My father's character reflected his origins: the vast, arid landscapes of northern Senegal, on the edge of the Sahara desert, a thousand miles to the north of Ivory Coast. He grew up in Dagana, a small village on the banks of the Senegal river. Everything there, from livestock to vegetation, faces a constant fight for a foothold on life. Toughness is a prerequisite for survival, and the practices of my father's Peuls-speaking Toucouleur community were designed to breed it.

For instance, at puberty, my father was taken along with other adolescent boys from his village to live in a forest that was considered sacred by the elders. Mothers spent years preparing their sons, drilling into them the importance of being able to endure the pain, hunger, scorching days and cold nights to come.

Finally, after surviving the forest, an initiation ceremony signalled a coming-of-age, the passing of a boy into adulthood. My father described how he and the others were lined up to be circumcised, one by one, in front of their families and the rest of the village, by an elder using a knife and no anaesthetic. The children had been taught that they must not flinch at the key moment, otherwise it would bring dishonour. Being last in line, when the knife had lost its initial sharpness, was considered an honour. They would all then leave, riding horseback, unbandaged.

My father chose not to continue this practice – mercifully, my brothers and I were all taken to hospitals to be circumcised – but I believe, inevitably, it played a role in shaping the man he became: one who could endure, who could be silent for long periods, who possessed an inner strength that prison could not break. It is no surprise that Senegalese soldiers were so celebrated for their bravery, as well as their intimidating physical presence, in the ranks of the French army during both world wars. 'You could give me a date and a glass of milk and I could live for twenty years,' my father used to joke.

Though his upbringing cultivated 'resilience' and durability – nothing in his childhood predestined him for the life he would lead as an adult.

Amadou Thiam was born in 1923 into a family of tradespeople from northern Senegal, far from the political circles of Ivory Coast he would later move in. His father – my grandfather – was a humble jewellery-maker and blacksmith; his mother a 'homemaker'.

His parents ensured he was born in the capital Dakar, which, in a quirk of the colonial administration, conferred him full French citizenship – unlike the millions of other subjects of French West Africa. His great misfortune was having a father who walked out on his mother to start a new family in neighbouring Mali. Without an education, and dependent on small remittances from her absent husband, my grandmother was quickly destitute, with more than ten children to feed and clothe.

As a result, my father spent his early years in rags. He remembers his mother wrapping him up in a piece of her pagne – the colourful cloth worn by women in Africa – when he first headed off to school. As a family of devout Muslims, he was sent first to a Koranic school, where he learned to read and write Arabic in addition to his native tongue, Pulaar.

The French school would provide his path out of poverty. The colonial educational system had no interest in and offered no prospect of quality schooling for all, but it was adept at identifying promising African children who could be trained and then promoted into an indigenous elite, always subordinate to the white ruling class, but with special privileges. My father was spotted early as one of these gifted insiders, and offered an education in the French system, initially near his village, then in the capital at the Ecole Primaire Supérieure in Dakar.

Once inside the French schooling system, he thrived. Primary school-age pupils followed the same repetitive drills and studied the same texts as children in France. My father could recite the verses of Victor Hugo's 'Oceano Nox' to the end of his days, and had the beautiful joined-up handwriting that remains a hallmark of the French education system to this day. There was no secondary education available to him and his peers, however. Africans were to be educated, but not too much.

In so many respects, he and my mother were polar opposites. If he was a taciturn man of the northern desert, Mariétou Sow was a vibrant woman from the lush lands and forests of Ivory Coast. We should never underestimate the impact of geography on character.

She was born into a multi-faith community of Muslims and Catholics; he into a family of Sufi Muslims. While he spent years in rags, she descended from a line of Akoué aristocrats in her home village of Yamoussoukro, an area populated by the Baoulé community. So many things divided them, yet they found a common purpose. They had first met as children in Dakar, where my mother had spent part of her childhood.

They were both fiercely intelligent in their own ways. They were proud and militant about their origins, and were loving parents to all of us. They trod the same path together for thirty-seven years, until my mother passed away in 1984, with quarrels and incomprehension aplenty, but with the bonds of love and tradition – and both were needed – keeping them together.

During his detention at Assabou, reading and writing were some of the only ways my father could escape his internal struggle: the boredom, fear and loneliness. On the outside, life for my mother brought different challenges. She had seven children under the age of fifteen to care for, including me, the youngest.

The families of many of the other men imprisoned with my father found themselves turfed out of their government homes. Luckily, we escaped this indignity. It was said afterwards that the strain of the evictions caused alcoholism and depression among some of those who found themselves in the street.

My father's role as French head of Radio Côte d'Ivoire which he kept after independence in 1960 had come with the privilege of a grace-and-favour home, offered by France, which we retained even after his arrest – the French union of radios (the Office de Coopération Radiophonique, Ocora) making the courageous decision to allow us to continue living in the house – and we remained there until we left for Morocco in 1966 – more on that later.

Although we had a roof over our heads, my mother immediately faced financial problems without my father's income, and had to beg family members for money. Fortunately, my father's cousin in Senegal, Habib Thiam, who by then had become a government minister in President Léopold Sédar Senghor's cabinet, came to our rescue. My parents had always been close to him, and had even taken out a loan to buy him Western clothes when he went to study in France as a student in the 1950s. He never forgot their generosity. That's the way 'social security' works for most people in Africa to this day.

Throughout my father's absence, my mother held the family together with her characteristic authority, courage and strength. 'He's in prison, but we need to carry on. We're an academic family. Be the first in your class, show everyone what we're capable of. Be successful,' she'd tell my older siblings.

All the while she contended with pressure from her uncle, President Houphouët, my father's former boss. President Houphouët was chief of our Akoué tribe and became the architect of the modern Ivorian state, forever associated with the independence struggle from France. A former doctor, union leader, plantation owner and member of the French parliament, he was in the early years of what would be a 33-year stint in power when he sent my father to jail. His and our destinies were and are to this day inextricably linked.

Houphouët would call my father 'Brutus' when speaking to my mother – his favourite niece, someone he watched over with rare attention and tenderness. He doubted my father's affection for her, as well as my father's loyalty to our family.

Headstrong and unintimidated – she was always famous for both – my mother would reply that she believed my father was innocent and that good men had been wrongly jailed. She contacted everyone she knew to intercede on my father's behalf, calling in favours and contacts from Senegal to Paris, including journalists at the newspaper *Le Monde*.

As a young teenager, my eldest brother Daouda took matters into his own hands at one point, bursting into Houphouët's bedroom and threatening him. We always admired him for this act of bravery, which we believe led to our father being treated less harshly. Houphouët himself was also impressed by this exceptional display of character – a desperate act from a fifteen-year-old boy trapped between his affection for his father and the authority of the 'father of the nation'.

The effect of all these events on me was different. My father was simply the elegant individual who stared out from the photos; a man who had existed in images and words, not flesh, since I was fourteen months old. I grew extraordinarily close to my mother as a result. I'd sleep in her bed, a habit that later led to a major confrontation with my father when he returned from jail. I was the only one of my siblings not going to school during the day, so I'd follow her around the house. When she went to the market, I'd demand to be taken along, devouring the mangoes she purchased on the backseat of the car before we got home.

My father's return in 1965 therefore came as a shock. Two years after his arrest, a trial was finally held, behind closed doors, and all of the accused were acquitted. There were various theories advanced to explain the original detentions.

Most people in my family believed that a senior policeman – hoping to advance his own career or possibly stage a coup himself – had concocted fake intelligence reports for the president, implicating Houphouët's closest and most loyal allies in a plot. In the tense atmosphere of the times, with multiple pro-Western governments like his being overthrown in neighbouring countries by leftist coups or revolutions, Houphouët fell for the officer's lies.

There were accusations that my father was involved in the plotting: a telephone intercept apparently included my father talking to a friend in which he said: 'I'll be back in a week and all of this will be sorted out.' He had perhaps said those words, but the suggestion that my father was plotting was pure fabrication. Many years later, a book suggested my father had been spared the torture and beatings suffered by his fellow detainees because he'd served as a sort of 'spy' for President Houphouët in prison.

The author alleged my father had meetings with the president while behind bars and kept a notebook with him. Only Houphouët and my father know what really transpired between the two of them in that period, and they took that knowledge to their graves. The book in question made my father furious, but there would always be areas of shade about his time in jail – mysterious places into which we were never allowed to stray as children.

This was typical of my father. The demands for transparency in the West have extended to modern family life too, where most parents and children nowadays live with an expectation of openness. I raised my own sons like this and enjoy the intimacy it creates. But my father preserved a sense of distance, protecting some parts of his life from scrutiny, afraid perhaps of judgement, or of losing his mystique.

When he stepped out of the car after his release, he was dressed in dark trousers and a white shirt. He immediately struck my mother as being much thinner than when he had left. As he approached the house, she and my siblings beamed with joy. I, a three-year-old, refused to even say hello.

Terrified by this unknown colossus – he was over six feet tall – I scurried to get away. For three days, I refused to go anywhere near him. Each time he came close, I'd run to a different room. Having enjoyed the undivided attention of my mother, I didn't welcome this new competition for her affections. There was no doubt an Oedipean dimension to my defiance.

It ended when my father grabbed hold of me and administered one of only two beatings I experienced at his hands. (The second was when I was seven, the day he tripped over me while I was reading comic books while lying on the floor, having warned me several times about the hazard I was creating.) Unlike many African fathers of his generation – and a regrettably large proportion nowadays – he did not use physical punishment to reinforce his authority on us. He was a man of letters and ideas, who favoured words over the crude power of violence. But on this occasion, he demonstrated the new hierarchy in the house in primitive fashion.

In lashing out, he asserted himself over a son who had not known, and did not respect, his writ over our home and family. Perhaps my lack of respect reinforced the sense of loss he felt in all areas of his life: the forfeited prestige, power, and self-esteem. I think he suffered more from administering the beating than I did receiving it. He gave me a 100 CFA franc coin afterwards, around a dollar at the time, by way of apology. It was a small fortune for a child in those days.

The most pressing immediate question that hung unanswered over our family was what the future held for us. My father's career had been one of lineal progression up to this point. He had succeeded far beyond the expected destiny of someone born into such a modest early life in Senegal. Once in Abidjan, he had sat the highly competitive entrance exam to train as a journalist in

France and join the French civil service, winning one of only two places available for the whole French colonial empire. This provided an elusive gateway to higher education in France, where he travelled to study, setting him on a path that would see him climb the ranks at the French state radio in Abidjan, Radio Côte d'Ivoire. He became the first African presenter of the news on air for the 6 a.m. bulletin, and in 1959 was made director of the station.

His arrest and absence raised troubling questions about the nature of power and politics in Ivory Coast and our relationship with the president. Back then, the discussions took place between my parents. But I would go on to confront those very same issues for much of my life, during a professional career that has also branched unexpectedly at times, like my father's, and faced unexpected interruptions.

In keeping with their characters, my parents drew starkly different conclusions on my father's detention. For my mother, it underlined the vicissitudes of political careers and the danger of being overly reliant on a single man, her uncle. For my father, hooked on the drug of politics, he wanted nothing more than to return to favour …

My father's faith was crucial, a source of strength during his incarceration but also of comfort in interpreting his misfortune. He had been raised as a pious Muslim who prayed with unerring discipline. There were the five-times daily prayers, of course; but others too before any major event, or every time we left for travel. He prayed before we went to bed, reciting verses on my head every evening. He prayed as he dressed himself in the morning.

The events, trials and tests of life were an expression of the will of God the Almighty. His hand could be seen in everything. Much later in life I would realise that having someone else in control of your destiny provides comfort in adversity. My father and I would later have many inconclusive discussions on this point. My own faith assumes a much greater influence of free will and self-determination.

For him, jail had been a test of his fortitude and of his loyalty to Houphouët, whom he felt had been misled and manipulated. At the first opportunity, he would forgive him. For fifteen years, my father would pray to be reinstated in his previous job as information minister. It was an obsession. Only this would be proof that he was innocent of the sin he had been accused of, demonstrating that he was pure of heart and deed towards the president.

He viewed Houphouët with deep personal affection and infinite admiration, rooted in their joint combat for the rights of Ivorians and Africans. He saw him as one of those rare figures who was able to bend history, shaping the lives of millions of people and a country in the process. And they both had a sense of mission, of serving a greater cause.

My father used to say he had spent his life fighting for the dignity of black people. It had begun when he first stepped off a boat in Ivory Coast at the age of twenty-four. He walked out of the port in Abidjan, and saw a white man coming towards him on the pavement, whom he passed without a thought. The white man stopped and turned around. 'Why didn't you step into the road?' he yelled at my father.

In the ensuing argument, the police were called. My father was detained and informed that, unlike in Senegal, blacks were expected to make way for whites and step into the road when encountering them. In the French African colonies, resistance to the white man's domination was often called 'l'esprit sénégalais' (Senegalese spirit). My father was left in no doubt that there was no room for it in Ivory Coast. If he refused to comply, he was told that next time there would be consequences. From this moment, he began seeking out the anti-colonial movement.

Houphouët came to embody the fight against racial injustice. He gave voice to the humiliations of colonialism; he channelled the frustrations; he held true to a vision of independence that was neither overly radical, nor indulgent towards France.

It was easy to see how Houphouët inspired such personal reverence. He had natural authority owing to his family background and tribal leadership role. But he was also quick-witted, immensely cultured, and possessed an uncommon ability to connect with people of all social classes.

Much of this was down to the decade he had spent working as a young doctor at the start of his career, in between the first and second world wars. Travelling from village to village in the westernmost part of the country, which had some of the worst infrastructure at the time, he saw with his own eyes the condition of workers and peasants, pressed into the service of an economic system he knew was unjust and exploitative.

During those years of crisscrossing the country, he built up a deep understanding of the people and geography of Ivory Coast. Even today, because travel is so difficult in many African countries, a large proportion of citizens know only their capital and their native villages. Setting out by bike or on foot, Houphouët developed an intimate sense of the daily lives of his compatriots that would serve him throughout his political career. 'Among the people, I'm like a capitaine in the rivers,' he used to say, referring to a fish found throughout Ivory Coast's waterways.

As well as a doctor's knowledge of the human body, he had a farmer's passion for the land, having taken over his family's cocoa and fruit plantations around our village of Yamoussoukro. I remember extraordinary moments with him as a child, walking around his land as he explained the intricacies of farming: irrigation, the importance of soil quality, the right conditions to grow pineapples.

His farming activities had led him into trade union activism and a fight for the rights of Ivorian growers to sell their produce at the same price as white rivals. From this spark grew the fire that burned within him, controlled and within limits, not blazing like that of other anti-colonial revolutionaries. It would propel him into a political career.

In the pre-independence era, he became one of the first African MPs elected to the French parliament in Paris after the First World War. His signature achievement was abolishing forced labour in the African colonies, with a 1946 law that bore his name. Until then, many colonial subjects had been coerced into a form of shadow slavery under policies that enabled white administrators, mine operators and plantation owners to conscript Africans for work of supposedly public utility.

After this, he became a minister in the French government for a number of years, before becoming the first Prime Minister of Ivory Coast, and finally president in 1960. As a leader during the push for Ivorian statehood, he always demonstrated a form of pragmatism and ideological flexibility that helped him bridge the clamour for independence at home and the French desire for lasting influence in West Africa. In parallel, his skill as a farmer and connections as a businessman saw his plantations flourish, making Houphouët one of the country's wealthiest growers. He bought a chateau just outside Paris, and later another in Switzerland. He owned expensive cars. But he shared this wealth with his extended family and far beyond. In 1950, Houphouët personally paid for 250 people to go to study in France.

Was my father, beyond his admiration for Houphouët's political skills, also drawn to this life of luxury and plenty? Perhaps. People who have escaped poverty exist in perennial fear of being pulled back into the weeds of their previous lives.

While my father's faith in the president was not even shaken by his arrest, my mother had a much more nuanced view. She loved Houphouët as her uncle and never stopped praising his generosity. But as a keen observer of human nature, she also saw the shade. She perceived the dark side of power, and the potential risks of a system centred on one man.

She sought to protect us, always encouraging me, in particular, to love him while never forgetting that, although he was my great-uncle, he was also a president. She used to compare political power to the sun. 'You never want to be too far from it, for fear of being cold, but never too close to it either, for fear of getting burned,' she'd say. She also sensed danger ahead. I remember her once telling me she felt like we were Jews in 1930s Germany.

After my father's acquittal, there followed a brief period of uncertainty. The family was reunited, the bonds of filiality restored between my father and my older siblings, and established in my case. I benefited hugely from the brief hiatus in his career, accompanying him for his daily walk to the Librairie de France bookshop, where he would pick up the *Le Monde* and read it cover to cover. We'd return home and sit together out in the garden, or in the shade of the veranda with its arches and fans.

In 1966, less than a year later, an opportunity presented itself that would satisfy my father's craving for professional redemption, and my mother's desire to put distance between her children and the presidential court. Houphouët needed an ambassador for Morocco.

Houphouët's first preference was to send his daughter, who at the time was engaged to be married to an ambitious and fast-rising official, Ahoua Nguetta. Sending a member of his family to the ruling monarchy in Morocco, headed by the new young king Hassan II, was intended to signal his investment in the relationship. Morocco, then ten years into its independence from France, was an important ally, one of few African states – like Ivory Coast – that was on a pro-Western, pro-American course, as socialism spread through the so-called 'Third World'.

In preparation, Houphouët acquired a sumptuous residence for his daughter in Rabat. But the plans came to nothing when his daughter broke off her engagement. Who might replace this illustrious couple? My father, married to Houphouët's favourite niece and seen as deserving of charity, was in the right place at the right time. He hungrily accepted the proposition.

My parents travelled to Paris for training at the French foreign ministry, the famous Quai d'Orsay. I was dispatched to stay with my maternal grandmother in Yamoussoukro, a period that I experienced as a traumatic form of abandonment. My grandmother was a tough, fiercely independent woman, with calloused hands from her work outside on her plantations. Uncharacteristically for a princess, she was absolutely determined throughout her life to be financially independent from her family and its head, Houphouët. I was expected to help out, raking leaves or harvesting cocoa beans. If nothing else, this rather unhappy interlude taught me to respect physical labour and resulted in me understanding the traditional tongue of my maternal family, Baoulé.

I was reunited with my parents when my elder brother Boubacar came to fetch me after around a year. We drove to Abidjan and the next morning, dressed in a blue three-piece suit for the occasion, I took a plane with him to Paris, before we all travelled on to Rabat, the start of a new chapter in our lives.

I came of age in Morocco, piecing together for the first time the various fragments of my identity as an Ivorian, as a black Muslim African, as the son of a wealthy family. I perceived in the attitudes and regards of others the prejudices associated with each of these components. I got to know Moroccans, but also white children and their families for the first time. All the while, I travelled back regularly to spend time with relatives in Abidjan, Yamoussoukro and Paris.

Our home was sublime, a modernist palace built by Mohamed Douiri, a Moroccan intellectual who had fallen foul of the king and been forced to sell. The garden was more like a park, full of trees and flowers, so vast that I could ride my bike around it and never get bored. There were hiding places throughout, under the lemon or orange trees, or down one of the multiple alleyways. The lawn was large enough for me to invite friends over for five-a-side games of football as a teenager. It was a paradise where I and my five siblings – my eldest brother Daouda had been sent to France to study – would spend hours playing unattended.

Perhaps because of this, and the huge pleasure I took in the attention of my mother while at home on my own, during the first year or two I skipped most days of kindergarten. My mother would ask me if I wanted to go in the morning, and would then indulge me when I said no. She enjoyed the company I suspect, in what was an alien country that left her frequently homesick and lonely.

A bit of jealousy, but also genuine concern about the way I was being raised eventually led Daouda to denounce my mother to Houphouët, warning that I was in danger of falling behind. A family meeting was called which took place in Switzerland. Both my parents had to promise to put an end to my truancy. Frequently, the president took his role as family patriarch just as seriously as matters of state.

This brief period was out of character for my parents, who were always so demanding and insistent that we all study hard. My father used to tell me in later years, anticipating that I would work outside Africa, that I needed to do better than my white peers, likening the competition I would face in life to a high-jump championship. 'If you need to jump 140cm, learn to jump another 50,' he'd say. 'Because when it's your turn, they'll raise the bar.' He expected us to overperform. I would later discover, to my sadness, that he had been right all along. This adage has been adopted by many ethnic minority families in the West today.

He dreamed too of children who would excel in maths or science. Part of this was pragmatic, but it said a lot about his own experience of discrimination. He'd argue that in maths, there was one right answer: 2 + 2 = 4. In an artistic subject, there was more room for subjectivity – and therein lay the danger: markers would penalise black students deliberately or subconsciously. Maths was a safe haven and, luckily for me, it was a subject I adored and in which I excelled.

Conversely, my father also argued that the white world accepted that some Africans could be artistic and creative. He liked to cite the example of Léopold Sédar Senghor, a poet from his native Senegal, widely read and admired in France at the time, who would go on to become president. Blacks could dance and make music too, of course. And their sporting abilities were beyond question. When you watched the Olympics, it was a wonder that blacks had never articulated a theory of their own racial superiority, he used to joke later in life. It was to our credit. All we've ever wanted was to be treated equally.

The scientific world was, my father felt, one of the last frontiers – an area where blacks had the most difficulty in being admitted as equals to whites; and he was determined that his children should try to cross it in the 1960s and 1970s. From an early age, he wanted us to earn places in the best scientific universities in France.

In Morocco, this ambition ran into the sorts of problems he had warned us about. My parents felt my elder brothers, all diligent students, were sometimes being unfairly marked down in class by dint of their skin colour. When it became systematic, and even noticeable to their white peers, my parents requested a meeting with the principal.

All of this was new to me – this world of bias and judgement; the idea that the colour of my skin could be a handicap. My siblings' difficulties at Ecole Paul Cézanne and then Lycée Descartes, the best French schools in Rabat, made it easier for me once my parents enrolled me there. They were popular with the local European business elite, who wanted an education for their children on par with the best schools on French soil. There were a handful of Moroccan pupils too, the heirs to politically connected families. I was the only black child in my year.

My introduction to school life there was brutal. At the first opportunity, on my first day at primary school, I was set upon by a gang of boys in the playground. At least twenty of them surrounded me and began pushing me. I was tossed around between them, my head snapping back with each violent shove. My newly acquired navy blue school jacket was ripped, the buttons torn off. My mother reacted with horror when she saw me at the end of the day. Another trip to see the headmaster followed.

I quickly made friends afterwards, however, and my scores were consistently high. My best friend Volkmar Schmidt and I would always be first or second throughout our time together. We were the best of friends but competed ferociously, driving each other ever higher. The teachers were committed and excellent. Only occasionally did I detect in the comment made by the parents of other pupils that a black child at the top of the class was problematic or difficult to believe.

I was conscious of sticking out in other ways too. We were among a handful of professional black families in Rabat at the time, along with the Senegalese ambassador Massamba Sarré and his wife and children, with whom we socialised regularly. Many people were curious about our status, while others were disbelieving. Even our housekeeper took years to come to terms with the fact that we could be wealthy and black. For her, black Africans were poor. Exasperated, but enamoured of her good nature, my parents eventually paid for her to visit Ivory Coast so she could see with her own eyes.

There were moments of hostility too. Every once in a while, bystanders would spit on our car, a sleek black Citroën DS, as we travelled from home to school or to the market. They were mostly the men at the very bottom of the Moroccan social ladder, labourers who endured a life of humiliation themselves. Black Africans were the only people they could look down on.

Any society built rigidly around the idea of domination based on class, race or wealth breeds these bullying reflexes: the weak, sensing their powerlessness, simply look for someone they perceive as weaker to victimise. The stubborn racism found in many working-class white communities in Western democracies is a different manifestation of the same problem.

Our driver in Rabat, Gae Dano Gilbert, had a special cleaning brush for occasions when we were targeted, which he stored in the garage at home. The sight of saliva splattered on the windscreen or dripping down my side window is not something I can easily forget.

Yet we were the extraordinarily lucky ones. I would sometimes catch glimpses of other black people. They worked as mute and downtrodden servants in people's homes; they strained and sweated as porters in shops and warehouses; or laboured outside under the fierce sun. Morocco's small black Gnaoua community – descendants of slaves, who are now revered for their music – were viewed at the time as clownish savages, as they went house to house to dance and entertain.

I don't want to imply we were badly treated in Morocco, which was the backdrop to many of my fondest memories as a child. We were warmly welcomed by most people. But I was aware from a young age that I was required to navigate through these different worlds and their challenges: the one of my parents, with the politics and power games of West Africa; Morocco, with its mostly white school and ambassador's receptions; and France, a more distant planet, at once malevolent and inspiring – a place I knew during holidays, whose gravity seemed impossible to resist.

As a teenager, I read voraciously, trying to make sense of them all. On the shelves of my father's library, I found thousands of books, literally – books on communism, the Arab–Israeli conflict, and a multitude of biographies, including of France's wartime leader Charles de Gaulle. One of my favourite books at school was *The Gallic Wars*, describing the Roman wars launched by Julius Caesar against the Gallic tribes, which I read in Latin. The intrigues and violence of Rome, with its plots and courtesans, seemed to mirror life in Abidjan and Rabat.

Very few people moved between my different homes and cultures other than members of my family: I very rarely invited my friends in Morocco to visit me in Ivory Coast, out of fear that they would perceive me differently afterwards. In Rabat, I was just the son of an ambassador; in Abidjan or Yamoussoukro, I was an heir to a political and tribal dynasty.

My friend Volkmar, the son of a German engineer helping develop the sugar industry in Morocco, was an exception. He came to stay one Christmas. He saw the family palace, with its moat and marble, its Louis XV-style furniture. President Houphouët gave him money and flattered him as a special guest. Fortunately, our friendship, built on study and football, was strong enough to remain unchanged.

In one significant sense, Morocco had much in common with Ivory Coast. Even though my mother was keen to leave the instability and plotting of her homeland behind, she found a country facing tumult of its own in the 1960s and 1970s. King Hassan II had to handle growing demands for democracy and economic development. Middle Eastern monarchies from Libya, Egypt, Iraq, and Iran were all overthrown in the period by socialist or Islamist revolutionaries.

Those were tough years, a period of major confrontation between East and West. Morocco, like Ivory Coast, being firmly in the Western camp, was determined to be a rampart against communism and Soviet-style dictatorships. Hassan II's political opponents were sometimes arrested. The father of a classmate was among them: a minister accused of leftist sympathies. My own father was also caught up in the first of several coup attempts on the occasion of the monarch's birthday in the summer of 1971.

Fantastically rich and good-looking, Hassan II was also smart and well read. He was relentless in his drive to make Morocco a modern nation with a successful economy. To this day, I have immense respect for him. My father was a regular guest at his table, building a relationship of trust over many years that would lead to him being one of a small number of people invited to the family mausoleum at the time of the king's death in 1999.

In July 1971, King Hassan had invited hundreds of guests from Morocco and France to celebrate his forty-second birthday at his beachside palace in Skhirat, a short drive down the Atlantic coast from Rabat. French VIPs and film stars mingled with businessmen, generals and ministers around buffets heaped high with seafood and meat dishes. Everyone had been encouraged to dress casually, and to bring golf clubs to enjoy the king's private course, or shotguns for clay-pigeon shooting.

Shortly after lunch was served, my father heard distant gunfire over the hum of conversation and polite laughter. He was talking to the Belgian ambassador at the time, in a vast indoor terraced area as big as a football field, with a swimming pool in the middle. The room had views out to the ocean through glassed-in arches. As a keen hunter and the owner of several guns, my father recognised the sound of weapons being discharged. Many guests, however appeared oblivious, thinking the noise was fireworks.

Suddenly dozens of soldiers burst in on the party, in full view of the terrified crowd. Some high-ranking Moroccan figures were called out by name; when they stood up and identified themselves, they were gunned down in cold blood. My father grabbed a chair and threw it at the glass separating him from the garden and the beach beyond. Clambering out, he took a bullet to his hand as the soldiers opened fire. Marcel Dupre, the Belgian ambassador, who had been in front of him moments before, was killed. My father ran along the sand for several miles, occasionally glancing down at his bloodied hand but barely feeling any pain. He eventually emerged onto a road where he flagged down a car and asked to be taken to hospital.

My mother, my siblings and I were away at the time, attending the wedding of my mother's only sister, Berthe Sow, back home.

President Houphouët was also in Ivory Coast, and was soon being briefed by an aide about the bloody events at King Hassan's birthday party. A news agency announced that my father had been killed, but Houphouët said nothing, not wanting to break the news to us until it had been confirmed. In total, 97 people lost their lives and around 130 were injured.

A year later, I was back in Rabat when a second coup attempt took place. This time, mutinous members of Morocco's air force – fighter-jet pilots – attempted to shoot down Hassan II's plane as it flew back from Paris with him on board. They strafed the Boeing 727 mid-air, killing several people inside, and knocking out two of its three engines. One (probably apocryphal) story has Hassan grabbing his pilot's radio and announcing: 'Stop firing! The tyrant is dead!', fooling his attackers into breaking off their assault.

The F-5 jets, roaring in the skies above Rabat, also swooped down to spray the VIP section of the airport with bullets, targeting the ministers waiting to personally greet the king on his return. The father of my next-door neighbour, Ali El Kouhen, a boy I enjoyed playing with, was hit in the leg, meaning he would walk with a cane for the rest of this life.

Hassan II's personal pilot, Commandant Kabbaj, pulled off a miraculous landing. I remember immediately going to the airport, like hundreds of others, to witness the aftermath. My father arranged for me to slip through security, enabling me to walk onto the runway, where I gazed with unconcealed wonderment at the royal plane riddled with bullets.

The attempt on the king's life was blamed on the then defence minister and army Chief of Staff, Mohammed Oufkir, whose wife had announced publicly and prematurely that he was becoming president, just as the coup was failing. Oufkir was later found dead, by suicide or execution. Hundreds of people were rounded up afterwards, including relatives of the plotters. I had been in kindergarten (and shared a bench for a year) with Innen Oufkir, daughter of Mohammed Oufkir. Some detainees were sent to Tazmamart, a secret prison specially built in the Atlas mountains, where conditions proved extremely harsh. It became the setting for Tahar Ben Jelloun's searing book about imprisonment, *This Blinding Absence of Light*.

Growing up in this atmosphere had a profound impact on me; the ambient insecurity took a toll. My father's arrest, the attempted coups, people I knew disappearing to be locked up in the desert ... all of this was real. It wasn't abstract history found in the books I read. The political tumult and instability of the 1960s and 1970s appeared to me in the familiar faces of people I knew.

At the age of nine or ten, when I returned to Ivory Coast for holidays, I would keep a gun by my bed. If an ambitious colonel or general with designs on the presidency attempted to take power with force, I figured there'd be a fight. I thought I might be needed and would practise shooting with my rifle, killing many grouse and doves in the process.

My mother always said that most African regimes were like a house of cards. She saw the fragility of their foundations and the injustices suffered by the poor. We knew personally so many heads of state who had been killed or imprisoned during these years: Modibo Keita from Mali, Sylvanus Olympio from Togo, Maurice Yaméogo from Upper Volta (Burkina Faso) ...

But my mother also insisted that we must manage our fear. She was convinced that many, if not all, bad decisions could be traced back to fear in some way. Her task, she said, was to help us grow into adults who could live without being slaves to fear – as fear was an inevitable part of life. It needed to be handled, listened to, but also sometimes dominated, and often transformed into a source of motivation and creativity. A person who could live free from the paralysing or corrupting power of fear held the keys to their own emancipation and happiness.

* * *

After twelve years in Morocco, we went back to live in Ivory Coast permanently. In 1978, having dreamed for so long of redemption, my father got his old job as minister back, thanks to President Houphouët. I never saw him happier, either before that day or at any stage during the rest of his life. He felt fifteen years of prayers had finally been heard.

I had already completed several school years in Ivory Coast from 1970 to 1972 and again in 1976, as our parents always wanted us to keep a strong connection to our country, but I now needed to complete my final years of high school. I was given the choice of going to a private school in Versailles, near Paris – the prestigious Lycée Hoche – or a state-funded school in Abidjan. My father was clear that if I stayed in the country, as the son of a minister, I would have to attend a state school for the sake of his reputation. Staying close to my family was my priority and I chose the Lycée Classique d'Abidjan. My brother Aziz, who has always guided me and helped me study, was supportive.

After the comfort and privilege of my life in Rabat, the contrast between the Lycée Descartes and the Lycée Classique came as a shock. Learning to study without air conditioning was easy. But I found it harder to accept that the state could not provide enough chairs for all the students to sit down in our classrooms. In my final year of high school, we spent most of the first term without a geography teacher. Other subjects were taught by people clearly lacking training. And this was one of the best state schools in the country.

I asked my friends in Rabat to send me their notes and exercises, meaning I was following two different programmes and school calendars. This felt like the only way I could prevent myself from falling behind.

Lives and destinies are forged in such moments. The most significant and unfair inequalities are the ones we allow to accumulate between children. Many years later, I would have an opportunity to tackle this issue by helping to build Ivory Coast's first new secondary schools in thirteen years.

My final school baccalaureate exams were also a fiasco, revealing one of the endemic problems of the state education system in Ivory Coast. Before going in to sit the final exam papers, many of my peers seemed strangely confident that they knew what the subjects and questions would be. Mocking those who had revised the whole curriculum, they boasted how they'd only concentrated on what they needed to. In fact, the exam papers had been leaked and shared so widely that the education minister annulled the whole process the day after and ordered all of us to sit the paper a second time.

I passed with distinction and my grades ended up being the highest in the country. I also won a national maths competition, which earned me my first appearance in the newspapers and on television. Thereafter, I faced a difficult choice – one confronted still today by many ambitious Africans.

Although my heart was in Ivory Coast, I knew that if I wanted the best qualifications and life opportunities I would have to go abroad, to France. This reflex had first developed in colonial times, when no proper secondary education was offered to African children. All my brothers had studied in France, including the eldest, Daouda, who was sent at the age of three to a boarding school at President Houphouët's insistence. The world has changed since then, with many wealthy Ivorian families now choosing to send their children to be educated in the United States. But at the time, all roads led to Paris, with its universities, its companies, and its promise. I headed there, knowing the expectations of my family and hearing the words of my parents in my ears: 'If you need to jump 140cm, learn to jump another 50' ... 'Science is the new frontier for Africans' ... 'Handle your fear.'

Chapter 2

A French Test

Heading off as an eighteen-year-old, I didn't conceive of it this way, but in retrospect my journey through France's society and education system would turn out to be a test of the country: a test of its ability and willingness to handle the diversity that its colonial history had created. At the time, I was just a teenager seeking the best education possible, fired by a mixture of my own ambition and family expectation. But reflecting on it now, more than forty years later, my experiences during this period were a fascinating social experiment – a sort of one-man assessment of the country's openness and ability to live up to the ideals of its self-image and national creed of liberty, equality and fraternity.

Throughout my childhood, my family owned properties in France, and we would stay there regularly for long periods every year. I took my first steps as a toddler in an apartment in Paris during one of our summer breaks. As a child, I'd visited thermal baths and natural spas, with their sulphur-rich waters reputed to help with asthma, from which my brother Aziz was an eternal sufferer.

I knew France through family stories and lived experiences. There were the tales from colonial times, a recent past, of my father getting into a fight after failing to show sufficient deference to a white man in Abidjan. I was well versed in the colonial contempt for African culture, the racist laws, the lost traditions, the resistance to French rule from my Akoué community. My maternal grandfather had refused to send my mother to school in protest against French values and colonialism.

I'd also noted as a child the way many French people looked at us, a large black family – sometimes a curiosity, at other times unwelcome – and how it made me feel. Immigration from sub-Saharan Africa was only just picking up in the 1960s and 1970s. France was in the midst of its long post-war boom, drawing in millions of new workers from former colonies, who came to toil in car plants and construction.

I'd also accompanied my mother on countless shopping trips to Paris, the bored child sidekick lured along by a sugary inducement or some other material promise. Like most children, I'd stare blankly from the chairs or velour sofas of the Parisian boutiques she visited, counting down the minutes in my head. I always knew I had to be prepared for a sudden departure, however – the first sign of which was normally raised voices, followed by alarmed looks on the faces of the shop staff. On other occasions, we'd walk in and then out with baffling speed.

She shopped in Paris as she shopped in Abidjan. No place was too humble or expensive for her. She'd buy vegetables just as comfortably as she would handbags. And as a proud Ivorian woman, she always dressed in traditional clothing, resisting the fashion for Western clothing. President Houphouët had even tried to ban her from wearing her 'boubou' in the presidential palace, an order she ignored as only she could. Standing close to 1 metre 80 tall, she was a magnificent sight, but not one that was always welcome in snobbish Parisian emporiums. At the first sign of hostility ('What are you doing here, madame?') or of sustained condescension ('Do you realise how much that costs?'), she'd turn on her heel, departing in a swirl of coloured fabric and angry French and Baoulé insults, dragging me by the arm.

In these moments, she would teach me the value of self-respect and of confidence. She'd give me lessons in the importance of being proud of our African identity, of not taking a step back when it was challenged. When people cut in front of us in the queue – which they did often – she wouldn't stand for it. She'd brought me up to believe in the importance of courage, which she viewed as the mother of other virtues: honesty, trustworthiness, and loyalty. She'd urge me to be respectful of others, to be polite, but never to allow myself to be pushed around. The stain of the slave trade in our past was a constant feature in the present. It informed her attitude and temperament. It was better to die free than live as a slave. This was a fight she and we could never afford to lose.

But I'd also been schooled in French culture and language. I'd been through the republic's classrooms in Morocco. I'd read de Gaulle's memoirs, de La Fontaine's poems, Flaubert, Balzac, Zola, Baudelaire, Apollinaire, Sartre, Camus, Giono, Maupassant and so many others. I knew the importance of Clovis as well as the battle of Poitiers. For all my mother's African pride and her passion for Miriam Makeba or Amédée Pierre, she also loved Charles Aznavour, the French-Armenian singer; Georges Brassens; Jacques Brel; Edith Piaf, and many others. After years of listening to Aznavour, I know every word to 'La Bohème', which remains to this day one of my favourite songs.

I arrived to live in France feeling equipped to succeed: I knew the language, the culture, the knots in the national character, the folds in its past. I admired France's capacity for reason, its love of the arts, and its passion for science – which, combined, had produced so many intellectuals and painters, as well as renowned scientists and engineers.

That was why, looking back now, I subjected the country to a test. Its promise to newcomers is made in explicit terms: the republic does not recognise or discriminate on the basis of your race, your colour, class or religion. In return, it demands that you adopt its values: liberty, equality, fraternity, and secularism. The French model demands a high degree of assimilation, making it very different to the ones I encountered later in life in the United States and Britain. But it was a bargain I could easily accept in return for access to its educational institutions.

I wasn't an immigrant who would struggle with the task of integrating or assimilating. I wasn't an outsider fumbling for a new grammar in a foreign land. I arrived with the cultural baggage already packed. Even my religious beliefs, so often a pretext for exclusion in France, were consistent with the country's secular values. Indeed, they were intrinsic to how I saw myself. I had been brought up as Muslim. I prayed every day. But I believed religion was a strictly personal affair – and that the shared human experience of Muslims, Christians, Jews or atheists gives them far more in common than that which divides them. Furthermore, my family could scarcely be more tolerant: half of my direct relatives are Catholics.

If culturally I was well prepared, what about socially and economically? So many Africans who have arrived in Europe in the last seventy years to seek work or safety have started off with only their ingenuity and industriousness to count on. They've built their own capital from the ground up, as my father did in Ivory Coast with only a primary school education. My privileges in comparison were legion and it would be disingenuous not to acknowledge them. My story in France is not one of rags to riches, of a difficult social ascension. The truth is there wasn't a significant cultural, economic or social gap between me and my peers. And yet, as I moved up through the extraordinary French educational system, exceeding my own expectations along the way, I realised that the republican promise existed more in theory than in practice.

For the one major difference between me and my peers – my skin colour – *did* make a difference. When it came to looking for jobs, I hit a ceiling pretty fast: it wasn't what I knew that counted, or what I was capable of doing. The only explanation for this was that my outward identity mattered. In the supposedly colour-blind republic, I was a black man after all, a Muslim, and an Ivorian.

As a result, my journey in France would prove fascinating, yet stunted. It would lead to great opportunities, yet always felt circumscribed, its potential unfulfilled. It began, however, in promising fashion ... on a sunny day in August 1980, in the garden of a convent southwest of Paris.

As part of our introduction to our new college, my fellow students and I had been tasked with cleaning up the convent's overgrown outdoor space. There was grass to cut, weeds and brambles to take care of, late summer pruning. Flush with enthusiasm and seeking to impress, we set about our tasks with excessive goodwill, breaking periodically to sit and chat, often in a large circle.

My classmates, smartly dressed even in work gear and neatly presented, were drawn for the most part from the most prestigious schools around Paris. They name-dropped them and bragged about their marks in the manner of young men used to impressing strangers. It seemed that many had a 20/20 average in maths and physics; one had even won a national prize in philosophy, another a prize for maths.

'And you, *Ti ... Tee ...* how do you pronounce your name?' said a boy when my turn came to speak.

'*Ti-dj-ane*. Tidjane. I was at the Lycée Classique in Abidjan,' I replied.

Blank faces. A few patronising smiles.

No one knew my school and I didn't expect them to. Sat in the middle of this arc of quizzical faces, I didn't mention the absent teachers, the missing chairs, or the fiasco of having to resit our baccalaureate because of cheating. Best not to give too much away, I thought.

My parents had pushed me to apply to the private Sainte-Geneviève school outside Paris to do what is known as 'prepa' in France: the preparatory classes which are required to pass the entrance exams for the country's top scientific universities – the grandes écoles. Founded in 1854 in Versailles by Jesuits, and nicknamed 'Ginette', Sainte-Geneviève was an educational hothouse, unmatched in its ability to prime pupils for the narrow and difficult path that led to famous schools such as Ecole Polytechnique, Ecole Normale Supérieure, or Ecole des Mines de Paris.

Described as 'every mother's dream' by Flaubert, Polytechnique was in fact my father's fantasy. Only a handful of black students had entered its storeied lecture halls, which had been producing France's top engineers and scientists since the post-Revolution era. No Ivorian had ever been admitted. My brothers used to joke that if I, the youngest child, didn't get in, my father would never forgive me. I was his last chance.

Privately, though, they were worried. My siblings thought I was too much of a 'mummy's boy' to survive the hardship and pressure of 'prepa'. The accepted wisdom was that I would last three months. My brothers Daouda and Aziz had both hated their time there.

After our introductions over gardening, my Ginette classmates and I headed for bigger challenges, the first of which was surviving the notorious hazing that all new arrivals were subjected to in those days. Inside the high walls of the school, an austere former convent building, there was a mood of grim expectation. All of us were boarders, most of us spending time away from our parents for the first time.

The first thing demanded was that we wear our pyjamas whenever we were walking around the school or taking our meals. We were told and made to feel as if we were in a jail in which the older students were the guards, led by the 'Z' – the elected leader of our fraternity. Anyone found in regular clothes could be 'executed' by a guard, which meant kneeling down in front of him while he broke an egg on your head or in your underwear. You could also be asked by an older student to do any number of push-ups, anywhere in the grounds. Showers were forbidden for the whole first week. This allowed me to develop a greater familiarity with eggshells than I could have ever previously imagined.

Other offences included looking at guards in the face. You had to keep your head down, sometimes on the desk if you were being addressed. We were also divided into groups, each of which had its own song with crude and often sexually explicit lyrics. A guard could summon a new boy to sing his song on demand, or any other arbitrary task. Failure led to more egg punishments. Needless to say, after two days, many of us stank.

We were given nicknames – mine was 'Lucky Luke', from the popular Belgian comic book series – which were written on cardboard signs hung around our necks, which also included details about our vital male measurements. Any older boy was empowered to check the accuracy of our notation. We were told we had to write and perform a show in front of the guards and older boys. Release from this purgatory would only come at the end of the week, after we completed our initiation ceremony.

That entailed waking up at 4 a.m. and performing absurd military-style manoeuvres in a nearby park in our now filthy and ragged pyjamas. The final chapter finished with us being ordered to crawl with our hands behind our backs through the 'Rio Crado' – 'the filthy river' – a nearby swampy area of putrid mud that was scattered with litter. In the evening, we were given a frothy brown broth concocted by our elders to drink. It was perhaps best that we were never told the exact recipe, which was rumoured to include dog food.

Exhausted, fragile and desperate for an end to the ordeal, we were then dropped in central Paris – still in our pyjamas, with the school hat worn sideways. Without papers or wallets, our task was to earn enough money to pay for dinner and return home. I headed to the Champs-Élysées – follow the money, I thought: a business principle that has served me well ever since. Through a combination of begging, windscreen-wiping and performing, I made around 200 francs, a huge amount of cash in 1980.

The induction week was a ferocious and brutal introduction to life at Ginette. At various stages it had deeply unsettling fascist undertones and echoes of the concentration camps. Some 'guards' even wore overcoats, mimicking the style of Hitler's SS. As a display of toxic masculinity and bullying, I've rarely experienced anything similar since. As an exercise in team-building, however, it was unquestionably extremely successful. It brought us together as a group. It smoked out some of the more pampered individuals among us, puncturing their self-regard and arrogance. It created what all managers and football coaches look for in their teams: a collective desire to resist and help each other.

I've had to attend many corporate 'team-building' exercises since that time. I used to dread the news of an upcoming 'away day' of the sort that sees colleagues asked to solve puzzles, go orienteering, or bungee jump off a bridge. The problem with all of them is that they are artificial, contrived, an incitement to phoney bravado and fake bonhomie. I never invested in them as a CEO. Crawling through the 'Rio Crado' worked because it really stank. Soldiers who have served together stick together because they've felt each other's fear. You learn a lot about yourself and others when you're running around Paris in egg-stained pyjamas. But that's not the sort of team-building you should or can subject an executive group to. I do believe in taking people out of the office or their regular work environment. People react to their environments and there are useful things they will share in a social setting that they would not express in a meeting. I've always invited my teams to regular dinners, finding the investment in time and money always well rewarded.

Then tolerated by the school hierarchy, the hazing at Ginette has now been confined to history for good reason. As well as breaking students – one American kid in our year never recovered and left – it was entirely at odds with the ethos of the school, whose values I learned to appreciate during my two years there.

Ginette was fiercely competitive: each of us was ranked publicly throughout, based on the results of exams which we sat every Saturday afternoon after classes. It was a bit like the NFL, bringing together the absolute top players in the country, except instead of yards or passes caught, it was the results of weekly four-hour papers on maths and chemistry that defined our pecking order. We also had a one-hour individual oral maths exam every week, one of physics every other week and chemistry every three weeks. But the individual academic competition was tempered by an ethos of shared achievement: the students in the top third of the rankings after the first school term were obliged to help those in the second and third quotients and give them two evenings of tuition help a week. At the end of the first quarter, I was ranked number two in my class out of forty-eight. Thereafter I devoted several hours a week to helping other students.

Time always seemed in short supply. The curriculum moved fast. Each lesson was conducted in typical French magisterial style, six days a week. Professors lectured us from the front of sparsely decorated classrooms. We'd scribble down notes as fast as we could, which we'd decipher later when back in our lodgings, where we slept usually two to a room. I had the misfortune of being allocated to one of the few rooms that had three students in a cramped space. Each person had a bed and a desk. We had a sink but no hot water in my building, Saint Joseph. By the second month, I had stopped showering systematically every morning in order to gain time. Some of my friends said they slept in their clothes for the same reason.

The daily diet of maths, physics and chemistry, as well as French, English, philosophy and industrial design, was relentless and gruelling. If you fell sick, you fell behind, sometimes permanently. There was no way you could catch up. We'd wake up every day at 7 a.m. and worked until 10 p.m., when a supervisor would come round and tell us to put the books down and switch off the lights, like a prison night warden checking on the inmates. This 'prepa' culture of intense pressure and overworking permeates and pollutes the working culture in the upper levels of many French companies to this day.

I liked other aspects of the school, however. The Jesuits emphasised the importance of self-governance before such things were fashionable, empowering students to represent their peers in various bodies that interacted with the school authorities. It was also highly tolerant, never exerting religious pressure. We were several Muslim students in the school, mostly from North and West Africa. The Jesuits insisted that we got together every Friday and be allowed to pray in a special room, below the church. They also provided halal food at every meal.

I discovered too that not everyone was the scion of a wealthy, connected French family: my main competitor, the kid ranked number one, was from a modest family in the south of France. He had one pair of trousers, two sweaters and no money. He'd passed the entrance exam with ease, and the school had set fees in line with his family's wealth. That was a standard Ginette practice: the fee varied depending on your parents' income, going from zero, for some, to a hefty sum for others.

Ginette also encouraged the Parisian pupils to take in foreigners and people from the provinces on Sundays. I ended up being regularly invited to lunches in grand apartments in the 16th arrondissement of Paris, the wealthy western district of the capital that is an enclave for the moneyed Catholic bourgeoisie. I'd be the special guest around large wooden dining tables decked with crystal glasses, candelabra and polished silver cutlery. We'd chat politely as course after course would arrive – soup, salad, fish and fowl, cheese, and desserts.

The question of my race and identity hung there silently, unacknowledged. This was polite society, and they were highly intelligent but also highly conservative people on the whole. I suspected in many cases I was the first black person they had ever invited for lunch. That I could talk about literature and politics, that I knew their social codes and manners, was probably both reassuring and, deep down, perhaps slightly challenging.

I heard that some parents couldn't believe that their children were behind me in the rankings. Most Africans they knew at the time fell into two groups: the general mass of new immigrants who were making France their home and raising their children there. They lived in housing estates in suburban areas and were generally viewed by right-wing people like my hosts as necessary but irksome labourers, carrying out the tasks for which French people could not be found. And here also were the barely civilised 'benefits scroungers'. The far-right National Front party had been founded in 1972, eight years before I arrived in France, amplifying openly racist discourse in the country's domestic politics.

The other group of Africans was much smaller and was to be found sprinkled across the beaux quartiers of western Paris. It comprised the children and family members of Africa's post-colonial political and business elite, who had earned a reputation for being brash and ostentatious. I knew this latter scene, of course. But I had no time for partying, and felt temperamentally distant. During the Sunday lunch conversations, there was always surprise at my graduation from a high school in Abidjan, then almost relief when I told them my father was a government minister, as if I could be neatly categorised.

My whole time at Ginette was geared towards achieving the ultimate objective: passing the entrance exam for Ecole Polytechnique. I would be up against 40,000 people competing for 300 places. About half of the students admitted to Polytechnique succeeded on their first attempt; they were called the 'trois demis'.

The other half got in on their second attempt – the 'cinq demis'. I had always been studious and extremely competitive, but the studying was intense even by my standards. My only respite was going to the cinema on Saturday nights, where I could indulge in my life-long love of films by Stanley Kubrick and Martin Scorsese. Paris was simply unmatched for movies anywhere in the world at the time in the range of films available.

I told my parents I would sit the Polytechnique entrance exam once and if I didn't succeed, I would go to the US and do something else. I recognised the value of the education, but thought the system was ridiculously Malthusian and selective. I lost 5 kilograms in the course of the battle. In the good society of Paris, I still get asked, in my sixties, whether I was a 'trois demi' or a 'cinq demi' at Polytechnique, illustrating the French obsession with rankings. It's not enough being among the top 300 mathematicians in the 800,000 kids born your year. They want to know whether you were in the top half or the bottom half of the 300.

I consider the French educational system to have serious design defects, but one thing that must be stated in its defence is that the admission process for the elite schools is transparent. Everyone sits the same entrance exams, written and oral. At Polytechnique, the oral examinations are open to the public. Anybody can come and see you take your exam. The grades are made public afterwards. Everyone can see how you fared, and you can see your peers' performances. It's not like top US or British universities, where the process is opaque. In the US, no one knows what the admission criteria are for Harvard. In France there are no 'legacy' students who are admitted on the basis that their father or mother went to the same school.

That said, the main problem in France is that in order to be in a position to sit and excel in the entrance exams you need to make an extraordinary amount of personal sacrifice and investment. In other words, you have to be ferociously selfish and competitive. The system puts a premium on these character traits, which are often unattractive. Ginette sought to counteract them by making us work in teams and help each other.

Ultimately, although transparent and in theory meritocratic, the system amounts to institutionalised elitism. The prepa schools that provide the bulk of successful students are tiny. In my time, two of them – Ginette and Lycée Louis-Le-Grand – provided almost all the students every year who gained entrance to Polytechnique. They had, and I suspect still have, a quasi-monopoly on the best young minds.

The total number of students admitted is risibly small. You must have exceedingly high literacy and numeracy skills. For ENA, which trained most of the public sector and government leaders in France until recently, you also needed to show mastery of cultural norms, which are heavily determined by your social background. Not everybody will be able to tell you what their favourite opera is and talk about it for an hour – another formidable barrier to outsiders. The country has changed slightly now, with new pathways opened up to the top schools, but the essential characteristics of the education system remain the same. Its scientific schools are probably some of the best in the world. It still produces outstanding engineers and mathematicians with amazing technical skills. I've run into dozens of them at the highest levels of Silicon Valley and in banking in London, New York and Zürich.

But their ubiquity abroad underlines the scale of the brain drain at home. Many of France's most skilled workers are still leaving for opportunities abroad. To be competitive, countries need to hang on to the minds and skills they have spent taxpayers' money on developing. This holds as true for emerging African or Asian countries as it does for wealthy European nations.

France also has a system that devotes a disproportionate amount of resources to a highly restrained number of hyper-skilled graduates. This is wrong-headed in my view. What matters in the contemporary competition between nations is not who has the best minds in absolute terms. It doesn't matter if smart French mathematicians are some of the smartest in the world. What matters is how maths skills are spread throughout the population.

If we imagine a country's citizens in a pyramid, with the most skilled and educated workers at the top, the apex of the French pyramid is long and thin. And at the wider bottom of the pyramid, there is evidence that numeracy levels are actually falling relative to other countries. In the last international TIMSS (Trends in International Mathematics and Science Study) maths tests for nine-year-olds, which are conducted every four years to compare the performances of education systems in the world's democracies, France was the worst in the European Union and second bottom among the world's biggest democracies. Separate tests known as the Programme for International Student Assessment (PISA) have also underlined the country's weak general performance in maths and sciences, the huge disparities between top and bottom students, as well as how the system is one of the least equal and least successful in breaking the link between poverty and poor educational achievement.

I took the entrance exams for all three of the engineering grandes écoles, but I was aiming only for Polytechnique, the alma mater of a host of Nobel winners, pioneering mathematicians, engineers and physicists, whose names have lit up the history of modern science, as well as politicians and business titans.

After working and cramming to an unhealthy degree, I had a full week of written exams, with each one four hours long. I still remember one of the questions in my oral: it was about the mechanics of a fly landing on a sphere on a table. They wanted to know what would happen to the sphere and whether I could explain the interplay of mass, gravity and friction. I can still remember the outline of my answer to this day.

The results were posted two to three weeks later at Polytechnique, which sits on a leafy campus about ten miles south of Paris. I was stressed, playing over my exam papers and oral responses in my head in the run up to their publication. When visiting the campus for a medical beforehand, which was mandatory for all candidates, the university doctor had asked me: 'What will you do if you don't get in?' An old urban legend is that the doctor knows who made it or not and generally tries to prepare those who failed for the bad news ... This had been enough to send me into a tailspin of self-doubt.

On the eve of the results being published, I had convinced myself I'd failed. I sat on the stairs and didn't go to look at the noticeboard displaying the list. The painful part would be having to tell my parents. With my own children, I have tried to avoid making them instruments of my ambitions for them. But my father never spared me. My friends' excited cries informed me that my name was on the list. I had passed. I had achieved my father's and my family's life-long obsession.

Why did he place such value on having a son at Polytechnique? I can only conclude it was one of the many insidious sides of the colonial hangover, which has been gradually shaken off by each passing generation. It was still strong for him and his contemporaries. For men of his time, although they were proud nationalists and had fought for Ivorian independence, they had been conditioned to think of France as a touchstone, a marker of excellence. They had been brought up believing that France's top schools were the epitome of refinement and intelligence. Although they hated this chauvinism, it shaped their opinions, meaning at some level they still sought to be accepted. After being traded as slaves and told for generations that Africans were racially, intellectually and culturally inferior, it was understandable that they harboured a reflexive desire for revenge that would come in the form of demonstrating that Africans were equally – if not more – capable and talented. Emancipation is a long, multi-generational process. The mental chains of slavery and colonialism are severed slowly. Young people today are continuing and completing the work left undone by their elders.

Once I finally dared to look at my results, I sprinted across the road to the phone box, where a long queue of people shuffled forwards to deliver their news to expectant family members.

'Maman, I got in!' I said when my turn came.

'Really?! Oh my god! Are you sure?'

'Yes, yes, yes. I've seen the results. Call papa! I'm coming home,' I said.

When I spoke to my father later that day, he was still elated. 'People looked down on our people, our race, but you've shown we're just as good as them,' he told me.

It was as if my achievement had erased a festering sense of injustice for him: the son of an uneducated jeweller who still remembered how there were no high schools in Ivory Coast at independence.

'For a poor French family, it takes four or five generations to produce someone good enough to go to Polytechnique. We've done it in two and it's not even our culture,' he boasted.

For the first time in several years, I felt like I could and wanted to relax. I'd achieved my goal. It's hard to overstate the role of Polytechnique in France's business world and the national psyche. It's only a university, but it also holds the promise of life-long membership of a small technical-minded clique, like a Freemasons' lodge for mathematicians and engineers. Members look out for each other, personally and professionally, and in this kinship lies the basis of a formidable network of power and influence.

At the time of the Revolution and in the centuries after it, France formally shed its aristocracy and class system in the name of egalitarianism. The graduates of Polytechnique and other elite schools represented its modern nobility. Throughout my career,

Polytechnique has served as an icebreaker and a calling card. So many times I have met senior French business people and their opening remark is: 'Ah, you're a Polytechnicien too.'

My cohort was an extraordinary example of the career-boosting consequences of being admitted. Three other graduates from my time ended up running major banks in Europe in the same period as me. Jean-Pierre Mustier, a friendly adversary during games of pétanque, led Italy's UniCredit until recently; Frédéric Oudéa became CEO of Société Générale in France; and Jean-Laurent Bonnafé has run BNP Paribas for more than a decade. My career trajectory in France would be less dynamic.

I headed back for a holiday in Ivory Coast where the news of my admission was picked up by the media. The country has moved on since then, but at the time it was a major event for the first Ivorian to have passed the entrance exam. Senegal had a small handful of Polytechniciens; Cameroon one or two. Most francophone African countries had none.

In September 1982 I flew back to start my classes. We were greeted on the first day by General Jacques Saunier, the commander of the university, whose earthy military humour was refreshing and prescient. 'In Polytechnique, the number of dickheads is the same as in any other walk of life,' he used to tell students. 'But they are even more dangerous here because they've been chosen with great care.'

After the non-stop cramming of Ginette and the weekly exams, the pace at Polytechnique seemed much more manageable – just a few exams every quarter. The focus remained on the theoretical, esoteric end of maths, as well as physics and chemistry. There was little in the curriculum geared towards practical application or the real world. But we also had the opportunity to sign up for seminars, usually delivered by professors or visiting lecturers with extraordinary intellects. It felt like we had access to some of the brightest minds in the country.

I soaked up the classes of Jean-Marie Domenach, a philosopher and former member of the French resistance during the Second World War. Marc Ferro, a renowned historian, was an expert on the history of cinema and delivered virtuoso sessions that opened my eyes further to the cultural and social significance of film. As one of the most politically minded students, I made sure I attended tutorials of Jacques Attali, who was serving as special advisor to newly elected President François Mitterrand.

Many of our lecturers were quite left-wing, reflecting the traditional bias within academia but also the wider political mood of the country at the time. France was undergoing a socialist transformation as I entered Polytechnique in 1982. Mitterrand had been elected the year before, in what was a historic tipping point for the left, which for so long had been a divided and therefore marginal force in French politics. Only in fleeting moments had it held power over the previous century, with Mitterrand's alliance with the Communist Party key to his success.

I spent hours discussing the 1981 presidential election with my father. Politics and international relations continued to animate our family life. Policy and palace intrigue, relations with France, the coups and instability in countries neighbouring Ivory Coast, as well as the latest developments in the Cold War, were regular topics whenever we got together.

I took a very dim view of Mitterrand's politics. I had read Marx and Engels's *Communist Manifesto* by the age of fourteen and loved it. The aspiration for dignity and equality it contained appealed to my young idealism. I even knew parts of it by heart. My father had once been a card-carrying communist, when the party was the main domestic critic of colonialism in France. From its creation in 1946 until 1954, the PDCI was a communist party and Houphouët-Boigny sat within the communist group in the French parliament.

Reading the *Manifesto* had spurred me to take a closer interest in the Soviet Union. But by my late teens, I had lost any sense of ideological fervour – just as the communists were entering Mitterrand's government in France. The shift in my attitudes was brought about principally by stories of political repression by the Kremlin, as well as doubts about the reality of the communist economic programme. I read books by Arthur Koestler, and dissident writer Aleksandr Solzhenitsyn's *Gulag Archipelago* and *One Day in the Life of Ivan Denisovich*. The lack of respect for human rights, the inhumanity, but also the corruption and incompetence of the Soviet systems, turned me into a free-marketeer. I threw myself with delight into the study of economics, with a particular interest in Milton Friedman.

I was appalled by Mitterrand's mismanagement of the French economy. He had come to power having promised a 'rupture' with the capitalist system, and formed a government containing four communist ministers. Together, they nationalised great swathes of the economy, including all the major banks still in private hands, as well as companies in steel, chemicals and electronics. The state was now responsible for making everything from food mixers to concrete. They also hiked the minimum wage by 10 per cent, put in wealth taxes, and increased benefits, all in the name of greater workers' rights and eradicating poverty.

I was in favour of both of these latter causes, but I already knew enough about economics to sense that the measures being proposed would be counterproductive. Those policies led to three devaluations of the French franc in close succession between 1981 and 1983. The government had to implement strict capital controls, like an Eastern bloc country. We were issued 'carnets de change' and were only allowed 2,000 francs ($400) of foreign exchange per annum per citizen. Mitterrand had been elected on a promise to create millions of jobs but during this time, unemployment, which was already high, rose to unprecedented levels. Growth fell. Government debt ballooned. Capital fled the country.

Like many young adults of the era, my political conscience was moulded by events such as these, as well as what I saw developing in the United States and Britain, which at the start of the 1980s were moving in the opposite direction under President Ronald Reagan and Prime Minister Margaret Thatcher. I didn't agree with everything they were doing – I disliked the brutal tactics – but their economic philosophy, their promotion of private industry and suspicion of state control, chimed with my own developing convictions, which were resolutely unfashionable for a student at the time.

There were endless debates on campus about who was right: Thatcher and Reagan – or Mitterrand. I argued for the former, bolstering my reputation as an Atlanticist by buying an Apple computer in 1982.

I could only ever embrace the anglophone leaders partly, however. Both shielded the Apartheid regime in South Africa by refusing to implement trade sanctions. Both engaged with characters like Prime Minister P. W. Botha, offering diplomatic cover for his institutionalised racism. Thatcher, who continually defied pressure from other African nations within the Commonwealth, even called the African National Congress a 'typical terrorist organisation'. Her treatment of Irish republican prisoner Bobby Sands and striking UK miners similarly appalled me.

Although I didn't vote, having not claimed my father's French citizenship, I found myself in a situation faced by many non-white citizens of Western countries today who hold similar pro-market and pro-capitalist views to me: the parties that defend these ideas tend to be the traditional parties of business, whose core support is highly conservative small company owners. In many countries, it's difficult to find parties which are both pro-business and hold a pluralistic view of society.

Racism was increasingly on my mind in my early twenties, and the more time I spent in Paris. I was happy at Polytechnique. I had my own space, a small room with a stereo and television. It was far more comfortable than the shared quarters of Ginette. I never sensed any discrimination or racism from the lecturers or my peers. But the outside world offered me regular lessons in how I was viewed by many French people and treated by the republic's institutions.

I remember driving back to the school one evening with a friend of mine, Piloix. He was the playmaker in our basketball team. I've always loved the sport and I think our team back then was the best I've ever experienced. Two of my teammates had played at national level. Piloix was charming, thoughtful, from Marseille, and – a detail that is relevant to this anecdote – white.

We were driving home after a game. I was at the wheel of my car, a two-door BMW and Piloix was in the passenger seat. We encountered a classic French traffic control being performed by the police. Of course they stopped me. I was black and driving a BMW. They always stopped me. In our first exchanges, they were rude, as usual.

'Tes papiers [your papers],' said the officer as he leaned in through the window. He didn't say please, and he used the informal 'tes' pronoun when asking for my identity document instead of the respectful 'Monsieur' or 'vos'. I handed over my papers dutifully, as well as the registration document for the car.

Having checked me over and walked around the car looking for a fault that would have justified giving me a fine or warning, he signalled for me to go with an expression that was a mix of hostility and disappointment.

Then, as I was about to drive away, he spotted the Polytechnique sticker that we all had on our windshields.

'Oh, you study at Polytechnique?'

And then everything changed. I was okay again, although still just as black, and still driving a BMW.

I wound the window up, eased away and exhaled heavily. Piloix was visibly shaken.

'I can't believe he talked to you like that,' he said.

'That's what it's like, every time,' I replied.

'I had no idea.'

In France, police are able to order identity checks at any time. They don't need to have grounds for suspicion or a pretext. They can pull pedestrians over at random in the street or drivers in their vehicles and ask for papers. Unsurprisingly, brown people bear the greatest burden of these; but racial statistics being illegal in France, it is not possible to document the issue, which we all know is huge. In Britain, such statistics are published every year and I believe they make British democracy stronger, not weaker.

Piloix's reaction of surprise and shame was the embodiment of Atticus Finch's famous line from *To Kill a Mockingbird* – 'You never really understand a person until you … climb into his skin and walk around in it.' For him, police officers were polite guardians of order who carried out their jobs bravely and unobtrusively. Like the vast majority of white people, he'd never been stopped at a checkpoint.

I've lost count of the number of times I've been pulled over while driving in France. Whenever I see a police car I reflexively prepare for it; I always have my papers ready. Flying to and from Abidjan to visit my parents as a student, I'd be regularly hauled out of line at passport control and interrogated brusquely. It even happened when I was a child. Once when I was flying alone, at the age of seven, I was detained and called a 'coyote' by an immigration official at Paris's Orly airport.

This gap between how white people and people of colour experience security forces explains to a large extent the incredibly polarised views on police violence in many Western countries. I no longer drive at all in the United States, having had one too many unpleasant episodes with nervous pumped-up cops drawing their weapons. Many white people find it hard to imagine a police officer being rude or aggressive to them. The de facto social and ethnic segregation that exists in many cities also means that there are few opportunities to correct these misconceptions. It took a trip with a black classmate and basketball teammate for Piloix to understand.

On the whole, my student experiences in France with the police or immigration services were intimidating, sometimes enraging, but remained fairly predictable. Having visited France regularly and heard the stories of my brothers, I knew what to expect. What I was much less prepared for was my first encounter with the jobs market when it came to trying to enter the business world for the first time.

After Polytechnique and two years of theoretical maths and science, I progressed to the Ecole des Mines in Paris, another top engineering school that was geared towards preparing students for the industrial sector. As well as studying the mechanics of turbines, for example, we had modules on accounting, law, finance, and chemical engineering. In typical French fashion, a lot of absolutely fascinating courses were delivered by some of the brightest minds alive, such as Maurice Allais, an alumnus who taught and received the Nobel prize for economics. The college was also located right next to the beautiful Luxembourg gardens in the heart of Left Bank Paris.

At the end of the first year, we had to find an internship. Some of my peers were interested in research institutions, others academia, but many had their eyes on the private sector. Like them, I wrote letters to the HR departments of major corporations in the typical style of an earnest, ambitious student. But while my classmates seemed to get instant enthusiastic replies, I was left waiting.

My anxiety grew as I heard them discussing weighing up offers, their dilemmas born of abundance. I quietly worried that I was doing something wrong. Perhaps some companies might have second thoughts about employing a Polytechnicien called Tidjane

Thiam, who had been to high school in Morocco and Ivory Coast – but surely not all of them?

But I never received a single offer. My letters went unanswered. It forced me to do something I had resolved to avoid, and which pains me to admit now, all these years later. I rang my father for help. Even though I had an overwhelming desire to succeed on my own merits, my sense of pride was eclipsed by fear of embarrassment.

Speaking from Abidjan, my father expressed sympathy and said he would make a few calls. He also knew of the emotional difficulties I was facing at the time, as we both looked to recover from the passing of my mother, who had died at the age of just fifty-three.

She had been suffering from a blood disease, which was never fully diagnosed, despite her having some of the best care available at the Paul-Brousse Hospital near Paris. I went to see her every day as her health deteriorated. She died with President Houphouët holding her hand by the side of the bed.

Losing my mother in my early twenties – someone who had taught me so much about our African heritage, about self-respect, about the importance of personal integrity – was a devastating blow. Houphouët likened her to a canari, a traditional African pot used to keep cool, fresh drinking water: 'Atoun,' as he affectionately called her, 'was the canari where we all came to quench our thirst,' he said afterwards. 'Our family will never be the same after this tragedy.'

He was right. I still think about her and am inspired by her wisdom regularly now, forty years later. At the time, I threw myself into my work as a distraction and the difficulty I faced in finding an internship was an unwelcome hindrance.

Thanks to my father, I was finally offered work experience through a friend of his who knew influential people in a large French company. For me this represented a complete breakdown of the supposedly meritocratic French model. I had had to use my dad's contacts to find a position when all my classmates found them without any difficulty.

I finished top of my year at the Ecole des Mines. Before graduating, I sent out another stream of letters looking for work: to energy companies, to banks and insurance companies, to construction companies, mining companies, steel-makers. My French contemporaries seemed to have a dozen options. The only company that expressed interest in me was the Swiss food giant Nestlé, which flew me to their headquarters in Vevey and offered me a well-paid position on their graduate trainee scheme. Not a single French company offered me anything.

It seemed obvious to me at the age of twenty-three that I would always be seen first and foremost as an African and a black man, which were disqualifying characteristics in the eyes of many French recruiters. Many years later, I would eventually leave France to seek opportunities elsewhere, feeling a mixture of disappointment and disgust.

And this returns me to the point I made at the start of the chapter about testing France. I had the same qualifications, the same education as my peers. We were drawn from similar social and economic backgrounds. Culturally I was mixed of course, but I had an intimate knowledge of France. My main distinction was skin colour. I thought to myself: 'If I can't get a job, with two degrees from some of the top universities in Paris, what chances are there for other black people in France?' And I didn't have the additional disadvantage of applying with an address from a working-class area in a high-crime neighbourhood.

What remains infuriating is the difficulty France has in talking about race and racism. It still likes to think of itself as the birthplace of universal values and human rights. Its constitution supposedly guarantees equality to all. Its lawmakers even removed the word 'race' from it because, according to former president François Hollande: 'There is no place in the republic for race.'

The idea of systemic racism remains highly contested in the country, rejected by many conservatives as being somehow a 'woke' concept rather a reality encountered and documented by millions of people. You can tune into radio or TV on any given evening and hear the sophistry of commentators and philosophers as they continue to argue that discrimination, insofar as it exists, occurs on the basis of class or educational attainment in France, but not race.

Nowadays, social scientists are able to prove what I experienced with data. They conduct experiments in which they send out near-identical CVs – one with a foreign name, and another with a native-sounding one; or they switch the addresses, one from a fashionable middle-class area and the other from a stigmatised district. The results are always illuminating.

Feeling despondent, I confided in the dean of admissions at the Ecole des Mines, someone I respected. He had experience in Africa and took a particular interest in the careers of foreign students. He suggested I might be a better fit with 'les anglosaxons' (English speakers). One of the corporations he suggested was the American consultancy firm McKinsey, which had begun selecting a small handful of graduates from the university each year. Though its prestige has fallen somewhat since, it was said at the time that McKinsey was one of the three most influential organisations in the world – alongside the US marines and the Jesuits. It was an elite institution that kept a low profile deliberately, while exerting huge influence behind the scenes as it advised companies and poli-cymakers. You couldn't call or contact them directly, but the dean had recommended me.

'Do you have any black people in your offices in Paris?' I asked when I was called for an interview.

No, but we're looking to diversify our workforce.

'What about if a client said they didn't want to work with a black consultant?'

We wouldn't work with them, came the reply.

I felt reassured. They ran a competitive, transparent process. They had asked each of the Ecoles des Mines, Ecole des Ponts et Chaussées, and Ecole des Telecoms – the top technical universities – to provide them with five names. We were all assessed and had to pass about thirty interviews each. They told us at the end of the process that they would award one scholarship for a two-year programme.

This was in March 1986. By this point I had given up on France and was determined to go to America and get my MBA there. Indeed, I had already been accepted at Wharton, the business school, and was thrilled at the prospect.

But McKinsey intrigued me. They offered to pay for me to study for an MBA at the business school INSEAD at Fontainebleau, south of Paris. They were offering the MBA, a salary on top of that, and if you decided to walk away at the end of two years there was nothing to pay back. I went through the process and was lucky enough to be offered the scholarship.

I gave up my place at Wharton and on 1 September 1986 joined the McKinsey Fellows Programme. One of my first engagements was working on a project at a French aluminium maker. I took part in a presentation to its CEO. It didn't escape me that I was now offering highly paid advice to a company that only a few months ago had failed to reply to my letters. This pattern continued throughout my time in McKinsey.

The consultancy was an incredible training ground. Not only was I completing my MBA in a class that contained forty different nationalities, I was working alongside consultants who were unrivalled experts in their field. We worked in small teams, always at the premises of the client. There was constant supervision and feedback, as well as a culture that demanded we were one step ahead of our customers and rivals.

Even when in 1989 I went to tell my manager that I was going to leave McKinsey to join the prestigious Young Professional programme at the World Bank in Washington, as I was interested in development work, they seemed to have already seen the future:

'I understand why you'd want to do it. You're twenty-five and you want other experiences. It's a great programme. I get it,' the boss of the French office told me. 'But I know you're not going to like it.'

He offered me a one-year leave of absence.

And he was right: I took the job, moved to Washington DC and within six or seven months I was questioning my choice. I hated the World Bank bureaucracy, which meant filling out a form even to go to see a dentist. After feeling constantly stretched and challenged at McKinsey, the World Bank seemed flabby and complacent in comparison. There were too many bureaucrats taking tax-free salaries in Washington, peddling badly designed loans, and lecturing poor countries on how to run their affairs.

Apart from enjoying the most spare time I had had for years, which helped me hone my basketball game, the main development from my brief period in Washington was in my private life: I met Annette, an African American staffer working for a senator from Delaware (one Joe Biden, who chaired the US Senate Judiciary Committee at the time). Despite disagreeing on the merits of affirmative action during our first encounter at a dinner party, we hit it off on subsequent dates. We married two years later in 1991 in Philadelphia, her home town, in a church that had played a role as a safehouse on the so-called 'Underground Railroad' that enabled slaves to escape from the South in the 1800s. Around a hundred of my family members flew out from Ivory Coast, all of them well versed in multi-confessional wedding services. Three of my brothers had also married Christian women.

I left the World Bank after a year, as predicted by my former manager, and took a job with McKinsey in booming New York. My regular hours and spare time were abruptly over. Fifteen- or sixteen-hour days became the norm, including on Sundays, in what became one of many incredibly busy periods of my life.

I was involved in what at that point was the largest banking merger in history, and decided to specialise in financial services. It seemed a logical place for me to work as a mathematician. My view was that if you wanted to understand business, you needed to understand the oxygen of economic life. The experience would be crucial for my future choices in Europe.

As an outsider to the United States, what struck me most was the extraordinary speed of American capitalism. Sometimes we'd meet a CEO on the Monday to recommend a decision and it would be implemented later that same week. The turnaround time was so quick, even when it entailed laying off thousands of people. Actions that would have taken months in France seemed to happen almost overnight.

I didn't hang around too long in the States either. After three years, I started to feel disconnected from my family in Ivory Coast and Europe. Annette and I were newly married and thinking about having children. We headed back to Paris, from where it was easier to travel to Ivory Coast, and I continued my McKinsey career in the firm's Paris office.

I continued to enjoy interacting with business leaders I looked up to, and I was learning a huge amount about how to run large companies. I'd also helped set up a club called 'Cap 2000', which sought to emulate some of the established networking organisations in Paris, but for Africans. 'White people have them. We should have them too,' a friend who inspired me to do it remarked at the time.

At its height we had 200 young professionals as members, who would meet for a monthly dinner. The idea was to connect highly qualified graduates across different fields, but also to present a different image of immigrants at a time when the far-right was gathering momentum in France. I invited the then prime minister, Michel Rocard, who agreed to come to talk, as did Kofi Yamgnane, France's first black minister.

We'd discuss events in Africa, where many francophone countries were in crisis. Many nations were transitioning to multi-party democracy for the first time, including Ivory Coast. And our speakers would leave with a different perspective on the African diaspora to the one they usually saw in the media.

Running the club while travelling and toiling as a consultant meant my workload was incredibly heavy. An event on the evening of Annette's birthday in 1993 made me think about permanently moving on from McKinsey.

I was preparing a presentation we were set to make to a client the next day. I had drawn up the slides in good time and was due to leave the office at around 8 p.m. I'd booked a table for Annette and me at a restaurant that had a months-long waiting list.

But then the partner called me into his office and told me the slides weren't good enough; they needed changing. I told him that it was my wife's thirtieth birthday and if I didn't leave now, I'd lose the reservation. 'Client first,' was his reply.

Those words were the firm's mantra. They were repeated dozens of times a day and they shut down any chance of discussion. As in major law firms, when it came to arbitrating between your own time and the firm's demands, you were expected to always put the client first.

I called Annette to explain that I would have to cancel, and eventually returned home at around one in the morning. The partner had been trying to deliver what was needed for the client and managing the work–life balance of his team. He tried to make it up to me the next day by sending Annette a huge bouquet of flowers, but the incident marked me.

'I think I won't be at this firm for your next birthday,' I told Annette.

I was right but little did I know that it would not be for the reasons I just mentioned. Not only would I not be at McKinsey any more a year later; I wouldn't be in France either, which had been home on and off for most of my adult life. Events in Ivory Coast were changing fast and, unbeknownst to me, the time was getting closer when I would be able to put my training and experience at the service of my country.

Chapter 3

A Homecoming

In late 1993, I was sat on a chair in the cavernous main reception room of the Ivorian presidential palace in Abidjan. In front of me lay a casket containing the body of President Houphouët-Boigny. His coffin was bedecked in orange, white and green – the colours he had chosen for the country he created.

The man everyone called 'the Old Man', 'le Vieux' – my great-uncle – had died at the age of eighty-eight on 7 December. A procession of mourners filed past the body, heads bowed, some in tears, as we family members sat silently on one side of the room with state officials on the other.

Houphouët had been ill for a few months leading up to his death. He'd been undergoing treatment in France and then Switzerland, but no one knew exactly what he was being treated for. My last one-on-one meeting with him had taken place in July 1993, in the bedroom of his magnificent home on rue Masseran in Paris, with him dressed in pyjamas, as he was frequently when greeting family members. He had just had a meeting with the Israeli prime minister, Yitzhak Rabin, who had brought him a pair of Israeli and Ivorian flags, which he had placed on his nightstand. Houphouët seemed physically frail, but still possessed of the vitality and energy that made him such a formidable politician. We chatted together about the Arab–Israeli conflict and about African integration, about which he was always sceptical. 'Une association de pauvres ne pourra jamais marcher [An alliance of paupers will never work],' he'd say. It was his view that until Africa got wealthier, there would be no realistic prospect of African states coming together as an influential unit.

He asked me about my life, my career – probing gently, as he always did. When we parted, I had no idea that it would be the last time I would see the man who had had such an influence on my life since the day I was born, if not earlier.

I cannot remember who delivered the news that he had passed. I think it was my eldest brother, Daouda. I was in my apartment in Paris on the boulevard des Invalides, which was across from Houphouët-Boigny's residence. My mind spun immediately, memories and pictures of him flashing through my consciousness – like scenes from an old silent movie. He had been a mainstay in my life and the family patriarch. I remembered him playing with me when I was a child; walking by his side through our plantations, the dinners and parties; and latterly our chats – about world affairs, his career advice; the mischievous smiles while sharing some secret. He was so, so sharp. For me, he was a president, a politician, a relative, and a confidant.

I knew how his passing would affect the country once the news became public. He had ruled for thirty-three years since independence. For many people he was the only president they had ever known. At the time of his death, then in his seventh term, he was Africa's longest-serving leader, and the third-longest-serving in the world.

It was inevitable that a debate about his legacy would begin now. Journalists would rake over his economic policies, his reluctant commitment to multi-party democracy, his spending. Whatever his mistakes and deficiencies, I felt certain that no one could deny how he had successfully created and then held Ivory Coast together – offering it stability, lessons in religious and ethnic tolerance – when so many post-colonial states had fallen apart under the weight of their differences. But this, his greatest accomplishment, was now in doubt.

When pressed on whether he would step down and name a successor, Houphouët had always replied: 'A Baoulé chief does not retire. He does not pick his successor. The dead don't have a vote. He dies on his throne.'

When he did, it opened up what everyone feared would be a period of dangerous uncertainty for the country.

I'd flown out to Abidjan the next day, to mourn with the family. With our blessing, the government had decided to organise for him to lie in state so that people could come to pay their respects.

We sat in the middle of the reception room at the palace, which was entered via monumental marble steps. The ceilings were very high, easily more than 10 metres above us. One side of the rectangular room was all tall glass window which offered a wonderful view on the gorgeous, lush gardens of the Presidency for which Houphouët had chosen every single plant or tree.

For two weeks, people waited in line and filed past from 7 a.m. to 10 p.m. I sat on one of the front-row chairs in the section reserved for our family. Its thin cushion quickly became uncomfortable, but that was nothing compared to the discomfort of the Ivorians who waited for hours under the sun for a few seconds in front of the great man.

Other than the infirm or those given to extreme meditation, few of us ever have the opportunity to sit quietly for two weeks in the same spot. My life as a McKinsey management consultant was usually a blur of meetings and presentations with fourteen hours of work being the daily norm. I worked most weekends and took close to no holidays. But I sat there as hours turned into days, and days turned into weeks, contemplating, reflecting, moved by the expression of communal loss, eyes fixed for the most part on the procession of my fellow citizens.

There were smartly dressed office workers next to people in rags or on crutches. There were women from the market in colourful boubous, who had put down their trays of vegetables or fish for the day to stand in line. Drivers, labourers, teachers: all waited patiently.

I was no dupe: I knew how crowds had flocked to Lenin and Tito's funerals, often out of fear once state mourning had been declared. But this urge to say goodbye and thanks to Houphouët was spontaneous and genuine. After all, three generations had grown up under him, with the eldest remembering how he had abolished forced labour, something more momentous for the poor and the downtrodden than even independence. He had freed them from the whip, literally, of the coloniser.

But what struck me most was the condition of so many of my compatriots. The country had been in an economic crisis for a decade – and it showed.

When I left Ivory Coast in 1980, it was a relatively affluent oasis compared to its neighbours and much of the rest of Africa at the time. While it had embraced capitalism, becoming a top global supplier of cacao and coffee, USSR-aligned neighbours descended into a mire of statist control over the economy and dead-end autarky.

GDP per capita increased eight-fold in the twenty years after independence, peaking in the year I left to study in France. People spoke of the Ivorian 'miracle'. If Houphouët had died then, his economic record would have looked nothing less than spectacular. The country had the best universities in Africa, the best hospitals, and the best infrastructure: roads, dams, power plants, airports, all of it.

But the thirteen years since had been marked by a collapse in cacao prices, a doomed battle against global markets to get better prices for the cocoa farmers, and then gradual suffocation by a classic third-world debt trap that closed around us, squeezing the life out of a once vigorous country.

What was clear to me as I sat, day after day, looking at Houphouët's coffin and the stream of mourners marked by poverty was that his death would be a watershed moment in my life. My mother had always sought to keep me out of politics, but she had died nearly a decade earlier.

Although all of my brothers were working in business or politics in Abidjan, Houphouët had forbidden me from returning to live in Ivory Coast until I'd finished my studies. I was somewhat hurt by the edict; it seemed as though he wanted me away as long as he was president. He had urged me to study in France, supporting my choice to specialise in chemical engineering at the Ecole des Mines. My professional life was giving me skills and expertise that he thought one day would be put to good use at home. That day had now arrived.

At the time of his death, I had just completed more than two dozen interviews with Goldman Sachs and had accepted a job offer to start with them in London at the beginning of 1994. But the prospect of taking a highly paid job in investment banking suddenly seemed absurd. Before returning to Paris, I let it be known to people close to Houphouët's successor, Henri Konan Bédié, that I would be interested in serving the country in some capacity. I returned to France, threw myself into work after more than a two-week absence, and waited.

The following month, Bédié's government announced a jaw-dropping 50 per cent devaluation of the currency in a bid to pull the country out of its decline. Houphouët had resisted it for a long time, knowing the hardship it would inflict on ordinary people. I am told that before Houphouët passed, he had come to accept it as inevitable. It was one of the few remaining levers left to pull by the government and would deliver a major boost to the country's cacao and coffee exports by reducing their export prices.

In February, I flew back for Houphouët's funeral, held in front of 7,000 guests at the basilica he had built specially in Yamoussoukro. I was still waiting for a call.

It finally came in March. Returning home from a Saturday night out at the cinema, I discovered a message from Minister Ahoua N'Guetta, Bédié's right-hand man, on my answering machine. The president wanted to have lunch with me in Abidjan on Monday. I rang back to say it was impossible to come at such short notice; I was in the middle of a major project helping restructure the largest French insurance company at the time.

Peter Kraljic, who was then the head of McKinsey in France, granted me more time off. He understood perfectly my predicament: as one of the most successful Slovenians living in the West, he had been offered the job of prime minister in his country after the fall of the Berlin Wall.

I flew to Abidjan a few days later and did some more waiting. Two weeks in fact. Every day I expected to be called to a meeting with Bédié. Every day I spent faxing back and forth with Paris and chairing meetings over the phone, trying to keep my client happy.

After a fortnight, the pressure from Paris and from my client had become unmanageable and I called Bédié's office to say I needed to go back to France. I was invited for lunch the next day.

I had known Bédié since I was a child. Always seen as a possible successor to Houphouët, he had fallen in and out of favour over the decades. As speaker of parliament, he had been named president in accordance with the constitution. Our first face-to-face professional meeting was in a private dining room at his official residence, with the prime minister, Daniel Kablan Duncan; Ahoua N'Guetta; and the minister of finance, Niamien N'Goran, also in attendance.

We discussed national matters: the power struggle that had ensued after Houphouët's death that had seen the then prime minister Alassane Ouattara try to claim power; the devaluation, which had led to a jump in the prices of imports and was causing severe economic difficulties. Despite the obvious short-term pain, I said I thought it was a good idea, providing it was executed and managed properly. The state was nearly bankrupt. Our alternatives were limited. The key thing was to control inflation so that, for all the pain that it caused, devaluation would ultimately lead to a sustainable gain in competitiveness.

Bédié was an extremely quiet character, a man who seemed to weigh each of his softly spoken words carefully, and was outwardly difficult to read – in that way he was rather like my father. He was nicknamed 'The Sphinx' for good reason.

At the end of the meal, he leaned forward. The niceties had been exchanged, the food eaten, the policy issues discussed. We had come to the matter in hand. 'I'd like to offer you a job in my new administration,' he said. 'I'd like you to lead the DCGTx [Direction et Contrôle des Grands Travaux], but I need a response straightaway. Don't tell me you need to call your wife to think about it.'

Annette, as it happened, was six months pregnant and expecting to move to London for my Goldman Sachs job. The DCGTx was the agency that served as a watchdog for government spending and an in-house consultancy for all major projects. Its main function was as a state auditing service, designed to root out corruption and ensure public funds were being soundly invested. When used correctly, it had vast influence on policy and the provision of public services. The chief executive reported exclusively to the prime minister and president, not to any cabinet minister. I remembered my father always complaining about the DCGTx, which could end projects pre-emptively or sink them while they were underway.

Bédié's political survival was still uncertain, given the constant rumours about discontent in the armed forces and popular anger over the devaluation. But the job was huge. I felt I couldn't back out now.

'I'm a patriot and if you think the country needs me, I'll do it,' I replied.

Before the meeting, I had wondered what, if anything, he would propose to me. I had imagined it might be the reins of one of the major state companies: railways, electricity, the national oil company. It was much bigger than that. I would have responsibility for overseeing each of these sectors, as well as roads, forestry, airlines, mining, housing and sanitation.

It was both flattering and terrifying. My brother Daouda, who then ran the largest company in the country, the national refinery, joked that I had been handed the ultimate poisoned chalice, which he memorably described as the 'shit-stick of the republic': whichever way I picked it up, I was going to get soiled. There was even some speculation in the family that the offer was a form of revenge, that Bédié was setting me and the Thiam family up to fail.

The new president was a man in a hurry. Having asked me to respond to the offer instantly, he then sent me back to Paris with a demanding deadline. I had to return to Abidjan within four months, to be officially unveiled.

My boss at McKinsey, Peter, was sceptical, but understanding again. He asked me why I wanted to go. He warned me that the country was too corrupt to be reformed, that I would inevitably end up in danger if I tried to work with integrity.

Nothing deterred me and, with the greatest respect to Peter, I am glad I did not listen to him: leading the DCGTx would prove to be the most enjoyable job I ever had. My achievements there were tangible and continue to make a difference to people's lives today.

I left my chic McKinsey office near the Champs-Élysées with another promise that they would take me back if, or when, I needed them. They assumed that my second foray into the development world would, like my time at the World Bank, end in disillusionment.

I took over at the DCGTx on 20 April 1994 – which was Annette's thirty-first birthday (I had kept my promise to her to leave McKinsey). The agency's offices were in a former hotel in the upmarket Cocody residential area of Abidjan. I decided to do a walkaround, which a friendly CEO in France had once advised me was an essential day-one task.

I visited all the key buildings and went from office to office, inspecting every nook and cranny from the basement to the top floor. I shook as many hands as possible – there were 4,000 employees – over a seven-hour period, exchanging words each time. I asked to be taken everywhere. Unlike my pleasantly chilled office, I discovered many people were toiling in the sticky tropical heat because their air conditioners were out of action. Many of the toilets were backed up. The roof was leaking in places. There was one functioning photocopying machine for the whole building. Out of a fleet of 500 cars, perhaps a hundred were roadworthy. Worse still, no one had been paid for six months and the finance minister had told me I should not expect money for salaries, including my own, until October. The government was prioritising paying down the country's external debt, which consumed around 60 per cent of the whole budget.

I called an all-staff meeting the next day, which took place in the courtyard of the building, with a few thousand employees in front of me. I laid out the situation in unvarnished terms. The country was a shambles. There was no money, and we were not getting paid. But I made them a promise: firstly, I would be there every day from 7 a.m., with my briefcase, and ready to work. Secondly, I promised to fix up the offices so they could carry out their duties with dignity. If we succeeded and could show results in what we were doing, I pledged to fight for the agency and secure the employees their wages, including pay backdated to their last salary slip.

My first initiative was to go to see Western donors and beg them for help. I explained the situation: that the bureau was in arrears to so many of its suppliers that it was no longer able to carry out basic work. We were like a small business with a cashflow problem: we needed money to get going again, to pay garage bills, air-conditioning maintenance, office supplies …

The French development agency, AFD (Agence Française de Développement), offered me a loan, knowing the importance of the DCGTx, particularly in the immediate aftermath of a 50 per cent devaluation, and the difficulties I was facing. Their decision to back our work remains to their immense credit.

Within three to four weeks, we had salubrious offices again. Engineers who were responsible for monitoring the progress of major construction projects once more had cars available to them to travel to sites. Completing a day's work was no longer a battle against the mental fog caused by heat and humidity.

I then applied fairly classic management consultancy techniques to reforming the bureau from the inside. I even brought in a colleague from McKinsey, who worked for six months on a pro bono basis on a strategy and restructuring plan.

Despite the fact we were in charge of monitoring infrastructure projects across the whole country, I soon realised there was no centralised database of works underway. Furthermore, we had no way of monitoring progress or identifying the reasons for hold-ups. Although computing power then was not what it is now, I knew there was software available that would enable us to categorise and monitor projects: I'd seen visualisation tools when I was at McKinsey that served similar purposes.

Soon we'd developed database software that could tell us, for example, if an unpaid invoice for a contractor was holding up the construction of a section of road. It became so sophisticated that, with the help of the World Bank, we began selling it to other African countries. We'd also have weekly progress meetings with department heads around the huge table in my office, as well as at the prime minister's office. We insisted on including key performance indicators in new projects approved by the government, which was new for many ministries. For me, it was basic project management: what gets measured, gets managed. Systems, targets and a monitoring process: it was basic private-sector know-how, but incredibly powerful in an environment that previously lacked these crucial structuring elements.

When I started at the bureau it was like a large hospital with lots of talented medical staff but poor leadership; they had the skills, but were not being channelled correctly. There is simply no reason, however, why African governments should be less able to hit progress or cost targets for major infrastructure projects than any developed country. Prime Minister Duncan, a disciplinarian like me, was supportive throughout, and an invaluable ally.

In my first week in the job, I also asked HR for the payroll files and went through them meticulously. Out of the roughly 4,000 people we employed, I had around 150 expats on the staff, mostly in management positions. Together, they accounted for close to 50 per cent of our wage bill. The 3,850 Africans shared the other 50 per cent.

I looked up the expats: they were overwhelmingly white French engineers on lucrative packages. Many had second-rate degrees from schools I had never heard of. They enjoyed housing allowances, indemnities and private schools for their children, historic inducements offered as a way of luring skilled workers from France. But Abidjan was no hardship posting: most of them had been in the job for fifteen years or more, suggesting they were happy to call our country home.

The issue came to a head when they asked me for a 100 per cent salary rise in order to compensate for the devaluation, which in addition to increasing the price of imports had increased the price of flights back to France and holidays there. I replied that their salaries would remain the same and that, if they wanted to stay, they had to accept local contracts.

I had seen the cost of pampered Western consultants in Africa before; it was one of the things that repelled me about the World Bank during my time there. I had visited Rwanda in 1989, where the bank had been investing in road construction and was helping the country to set up a fund to pay for highway maintenance. My team was meant to supervise and audit the work of World Bank-financed consultants. The chumminess between the consultants on the ground in Rwanda and some of the bank's staff was immediately obvious, making any objective, independent assessment of their work impossible. We drove around in the World Bank boss's car and dined in his sprawling villa. His one-year contract had been renewed every year for ten years.

I believed this type of 'technical assistance' was doomed because of the built-in conflict of interests. The consultants were offered attractive short-term contracts, and they were supposed to put themselves out of a job by transferring their skills to Rwandans. Some people did that effectively, were often given a medal and went home or to a new assignment elsewhere. Others enjoyed the well-paid life in an 'exotic' place and strangely never seemed to be able to find someone good enough to replace them. Their fixed-term technical assistance contracts would be renewed again and again. I wrote a report saying that the World Bank should make all such contracts strictly non-renewable: either the technical assistance was successful – meaning local people had been trained to take over; or it had not – the mission had failed and the consultant needed to be replaced.

It was a circular gravy train in which Western development money was being spent in Rwanda, but then ended up supporting consultants who flew in from London, Paris or Washington. Today the system has improved, but even now too much development money ends up this way: creating a sort of poverty industry subsidy network, in which developing countries spend funds destined for the poor on Western equipment and consultants.

Out of 150 French employees at the DCGTx, just nine chose to stay. I had a visit shortly afterwards from a diplomat at the French embassy. 'I just wanted to know why you are increasing the unemployment rate in France?' he said with a wry smile. 'People are saying all sorts of things about you. We'd like to know if you are pro- or anti-France?'

'I'm just pro-Ivory Coast,' I replied, adding that I was taking decisions in the interests of my country. 'I'm sure you'd do the same.'

Having reduced the salary bill by about 40 per cent, I was able to offer pay rises to the rest of the staff. By the end of the year, the finance ministry was finally releasing funds to enable us to honour our payroll commitments, meaning everyone was receiving their wages, backdated for the previous months and at a much higher salary than before.

As the French staff left, I promoted Ivorians into their roles. Out of fourteen departments, thirteen had been run by white people. My two predecessors in the CEO role had also been white. It was clear to me that there were plenty of Ivorians with the necessary skills, training and temperament. But the hesitance I encountered revealed an important lesson in the importance of self-confidence and – again – the deep rot of colonialism.

In the agricultural unit, I decided to promote the deputy director, who was a top Ivorian engineer. Instead of being delighted at the news, he came to see me afterwards to ask suspiciously why I was so keen to promote him. I told him I had faith in his abilities and that he'd been doing most of the work already.

'I've been talking to people and they think you're giving me the job so I'll fail,' he countered.

I laughed. I said I was giving him the post because I knew he could do it. I've kept in touch with him, and he has since gone on to have a stellar career in the country.

Nowadays I often say that we Africans need to 'emancipate ourselves from mental slavery', to quote Marcus Garvey, which Bob Marley sang about in 'Redemption Song'. That is the last step of the journey. If we have inferiority complexes vis-à-vis others, imagining we can't beat them, or that their culture or inherent worth is more than ours, then we have built for ourselves a very effective mental prison – a prison without bars but one that will always turn us into losers.

Part of my new job at DCGTx was encouraging a different mentality – one of ambition, self-belief, and responsibility. I gave every new department head autonomy and targets, making clear that they would be held accountable. It was a major shake-up that was accompanied by a clear improvement in working conditions: as well as the pay rises and backpay, for instance, I set up medical facilities for employees and their families, as well as a pension fund and health insurance for everyone.

Beyond this internal reorganisation, one of my first tasks was to negotiate pay rises with trade unions representing staff in the state-owned power, water and other utility sectors. Everyone was pushing for major rises to compensate for the currency devaluation, which had sent inflation spiralling. But unless we could contain the wage increases, the boost to the country's overall competitiveness would be lost.

It helped being an Ivorian. One of the electricity company chief executives had previously refused to attend meetings at the bureau's offices because it was run by a Frenchman. I could meet the bosses of our utilities and speak to them as equals. In most cases, we negotiated wage rises of around 30 per cent, a manageable level considering the value of the currency had been slashed in half.

With elections looming in 1995, President Bédié was also concerned about the possibility of a power crisis. Serious problems were brewing because a drought had led to low water levels in our reservoirs, threatening hydroelectric production. Power provision is an extremely sensitive issue in Africa. Citizens will put up with many things, but nothing reeks of mismanagement and negligence more than the lights going out unexpectedly. There's a maxim in African politics that if you mismanage power, you lose power.

Bédié wanted me to oversee the creation of a new gas-fired power station. A US energy company had recently struck oil several miles off the Ivorian coast. Instead of flaring off the gas from the field, as was common practice in the industry at the time, there was a possibility of bringing it onshore to provide relatively clean and cheap power for our growing population. Because the gas was seen as a simple byproduct of oil extraction, we would buy it for next to nothing.

I had to assemble a team of experts and lawyers to carry out the technical studies. There was already a project seeking to bring in offshore gas to Abidjan for electricity production, which was backed by the World Bank. I set about trying to prove that the new oil and gas field, which was closer to the coast, would be a more cost-effective solution.

Our calculations suggested that the electricity would be around 30 per cent cheaper than the rival World Bank-funded facility. But the World Bank was insistent that the other project should go ahead. At one point, I had to threaten to leak a story to the American media that Ivory Coast, a near bankrupt country, was being pressured into proceeding with a project it knew was not cost effective. 'How are you going to justify that people in a poor country pay more for power than they need to?' I told the top World Bank official for West Africa at one of many tense meetings.

'Foxtrot' became Africa's first privately run power project and one of its most cost effective. It didn't cost the taxpayer anything and increased domestic electricity generation capacity by 30 per cent. The project took so much of my energy that I joked with my wife that we should name our first son Foxtrot. He was born just as we were finalising the contracts.

The project cast me briefly into the international limelight. Foxtrot led to a second, bigger public–private scheme named Azito, which featured in a list of innovative global projects in the *Financial*

Times and led me to be named as a 'Global Leader for Tomorrow' at the World Economic Forum in Davos in 1998. But Azito also caused me more problems with the French embassy.

Over meetings in Paris and Washington, I finalised a deal that saw a consortium of Switzerland's ABB and France's EDF build the Azito plant west of Abidjan, with funding from the World Bank and the Aga Khan Foundation. It was the biggest private tender in Ivorian history at the time.

By appointing ABB to build the turbines instead of the Franco-Belgian group Suez-Tractebel, the furious French ambassador informed me that I had 'ruined a hundred years of Franco–Ivorian relations'. I replied that those relations weren't worth much if three turbines were enough to ruin them.

I also explained how we had run a transparent bidding process and had a committee tasked with analysing the offers, which we received from ABB, Suez, and US-based General Electric. ABB was the cheapest. It was as simple as that.

Huge pressure was exerted on the Ivorian government by the French to reverse the choice. President Jacques Chirac even called Bédié personally and mentioned the deal. At one point, I had to threaten to resign when it looked as if my superiors might buckle. In a telling illustration of the post-colonial attitude and policy of France towards its former territories, Paris expected preferential treatment, even when it was manifestly against our interests. At one point, I was advised not to travel to France out of concerns for my security.

It underlined starkly how Paris, and many Western countries more broadly, say one thing in public and another in private. Outwardly, they all want good governance, transparency and corruption-free government in Africa. They lament the waste and patronage systems – except when their interests are involved.

*   *   *

In the three years after the devaluation, Ivory Coast experienced annual economic growth of 7, 8 and 9 per cent a year – the sort of rates that were common in the first 'miracle' post-independence decades of the Houphouët years. The country was still asphyxiated by its foreign debt payments, which consumed up to 40 per cent of the national budget. But the growth, plus new oil revenues, gave us a windfall of revenues and some leeway to relaunch essential infrastructure building programmes.

No new state schools had been constructed in the whole country for decades. We set a target of 1,700 new classrooms a year. There were new investments in water, sanitation, and roads. The entire infrastructure programme was dubbed the '12 Tasks of the African Elephant' and was meant to transform Ivory Coast.

For me, the job and agenda seemed ideal: it called on the expertise I'd acquired as a management consultant, as well as the technical engineering skills I'd learned at university in Paris. I considered myself to be in public service, but not in politics. I was also learning about the mechanics of running a country: the legislative process, the budgetary cycle, how to enact reforms or negotiate government contracts.

Although I was taking on more and more politically sensitive work, I was happy for ministers to be the face of the announcements and policies. As Harry S. Truman once remarked: 'It's amazing what you can accomplish if you do not care who gets the credit.' Working for the most part out of the public eye suited my temperament.

I was also instrumental in building what was the first proper mosque in Abidjan. Bédié, a Catholic, was seen by many people as being anti-Muslim, and a new Islamic place of worship in the capital was seen as a way of countering this reputation. He wanted me to travel to Morocco and the kingdoms around the Middle East to seek their financial support.

One of my abiding memories from the whole mosque-building project was the amount of time I spent waiting. In many monarchies, visitors are announced to the king only once. Thereafter, reminding the regent is frowned upon or, worse – an act of lèse-majesté. No one in the court is able to predict when a waiting visitor might be received, or even where the king is. I would spend days upon days in my hotel room, just waiting.

In Morocco, my father's contacts helped me gain an introduction to King Hassan II. He finally received me and my father at one in the morning in the company of the crown prince, Mohammed. Fortunately, the ten-day patience test proved worth it: not only was he supportive, he furnished me with a personal letter of introduction for the royal courts throughout the Middle East. He also offered his personal plane for me to travel on to Kuwait, Dubai, Abu Dhabi, and Riyadh.

After many months, I returned to Abidjan with pledges of around $20 million, most of it from the Emir of Dubai. That gave us the confidence to employ an architect, who drew up plans for a complex containing the religious facilities as well as commercial space that could be rented out.

One of the biggest challenges when building new monuments in Africa is budgeting for the maintenance costs that will be required afterwards. We felt that the best defence against crumbling walls and blocked drains in the future was to provide rental income that could be tapped to cover the service costs.

Before construction began, the designs had to be presented again to the financial backers, some of whom requested minor changes, again after weeks of keeping me idling nearby. I was gone for three months on this second tour of duty, causing me to miss the birth of my second son.

I was also taking part in negotiations with the International Monetary Fund and the World Bank, our two key multilateral creditors. Under agreements with them, we privatised around thirty public companies in telecoms, palm oil, sugar companies, and the railways, helping roll back the state from crucial parts of the economy. I played a major role in the construction of the first new bridge in Abidjan, as well as renovating the Félix-Houphouët-Boigny International Airport, building a new slaughterhouse, modernising the port, and constructing a multi-purpose Olympic-size national stadium. Of 'the 12 Tasks of the African Elephant', all but one has been completed.

In 1998, Bédié asked me to join his government, which would formalise my responsibilities that had become those of a de facto cabinet member. I didn't seek out the position, and felt like my influence and impact on the lives of Ivorians as head of the agency responsible for delivering infrastructure was far greater than most ministers. I reluctantly accepted being named minister of development on condition that I retained control over the DCGTx.

In truth, at around this time, I was starting to worry about the domestic political climate. All the economic indicators were positive: as well as high economic growth, rising private investment, falling inflation, and the public accounts were in their best shape in years. Surveys showed that poverty levels, which had been increasing for a decade, were declining. But President Houphouët's main political legacy was fraying.

Identity politics based on tribal loyalties and religion were in the ascendancy. The genie that had destroyed so many post-colonial states was out of the bottle. The 1995 presidential election that saw Bédié elected for the first time had been marred by violence.

His main rival, Alassane Ouattara, had been banned from running on the basis of a new law requiring that the parents of all presidential candidates to both be Ivorian. Ouattara's father was from Burkina Faso, and he had served as an official for that country at the International Monetary Fund (IMF). Bédié's other rival, Laurent Gbagbo, boycotted the polls.

There was also a serious problem with revenue collection, which tallied with growing public anger about corruption. Although the economy was booming, tax and customs receipts were not rising in step. There was too much 'leakage', as it is euphemistically termed.

The IMF became increasingly hostile under the influence of Ouattara, who was then its deputy managing director, putting us under sanctions and refusing to entertain any notion of debt-restructuring, despite the weight of our repayments which were crippling us again by 1999.

Internally, I wrote note after note to the president about corruption in the customs department, which was under the supervision of the finance ministry. Revenues from coffee and cacao exporters have always been a key source of income for the country. They should have been bountiful because prices had rebounded to historic highs.

Everyone had warned me before taking the job that I would end up tainted, that my margin for manoeuvre would be so limited that I would be at best an impotent internal whistleblower. I felt I'd proved them wrong. I'd worked quietly and efficiently beyond the scenes to stop as much waste as possible and introduce transparency in the bidding processes.

I'd prevented bogus payments and padded contracts and kickbacks whenever I'd had sufficient proof and powers to stop them. I blocked transfers to front companies in Italy, Lebanon and Nigeria, each time saving Ivorian taxpayers money. Every time I saved money for either the state or Ivorian consumers.

In the middle of 1999, with tensions growing, I decided that it would be safer for Annette and the boys, then aged three and four, to move back to France. The signs were increasingly ominous, with opposition demonstrations growing in strength. I became more and more disillusioned and less cautious in meetings with cabinet colleagues, expressing my opinions more forcefully, without calculation or fear for the consequences. I sensed that neither I – and perhaps nor they – would be around the cabinet table for long.

In late December, I attended a six-hour meeting with the IMF head of mission to discuss the agency's sanctions. President Bédié was there, as was the finance minister. Afterwards, I told Bédié I'd be spending Christmas in the United States. I hadn't seen my family in months and Annette had gone to see her parents in Philadelphia for the holidays. It was the last conversation I had with Bédié as president.

As I awoke on my flight into Paris the following morning, people back in Abidjan were trying to make sense of the sound of gunfire. Once I reached my hotel, my ministerial chief of staff rang to report shooting. He said there were soldiers everywhere. It appeared to be a mutiny. I boarded my second flight to Philadelphia. By the time we touched down, it was fait accompli.

'It's game over,' Annette told me at the airport. President Bédié had been overthrown in the country's first coup d'état.

It had all started as a pay dispute. Bédié had sent soldiers to assist with a UN peacekeeping mission in the Central African Republic. President Houphouët had always been reluctant to send Ivorian soldiers abroad. He used to joke that they would only learn how to use their weapons, turn into thugs, and get ambitions of self-advancement when they came home. Much better to keep them coddled and close.

The peacekeepers had returned disgruntled, claiming they were owed unpaid wages and demanding better living conditions. A handful of junior officers led the wage demands on behalf of their men during a dispute that might have been quickly resolved, but instead was allowed to fester. Their mutiny, when it occurred on 23 December 1999, sparked a much larger movement and gave opportunists in the armed forces a pretext for a putsch.

Troops took over in a drill that had been well rehearsed in neighbouring countries over the last four decades – seizing control of key transport infrastructure as well as radio and television headquarters. They occupied the presidential palace, where they met no resistance.

General Robert Guëï, a man I knew well, proclaimed himself to be president. Bédié used the French radio station RFI to appeal for civilians and loyalists in the army to fight back. Once it became clear that his efforts were in vain, he fled to the French embassy in Abidjan, eventually emerging in exile in Paris. One of Africa's hitherto most stable countries had fallen like others under the boot of military rule.

Christmas that year was a blur. I was on the phone constantly, trying to reach my staff and family back home, desperate for information. I also spoke to Susan Rice, then US undersecretary for African affairs, who had been a McKinsey consultant at the same time as me. There were about ten black consultants in the whole firm, so we'd got to know each other.

Like every coup leader, Guëï courted popular opinion by promising to make tackling corruption one of his priorities. Ten ministers were rounded up and locked in a military barracks close to Abidjan.

After around three days, I told Annette I needed to go to Paris. The time difference between Abidjan and Philadelphia was impossible to manage and I wanted to see people who were informed on what was going on back home. She pleaded with me to stay.

'I have to go. I can't do anything from here,' I said.

During my transatlantic flight I had plenty of time to contemplate my decision: the ruined holiday after such a long separation; leaving the boys without knowing when I would see them again. Was it worth it? How much did I value my career, my safety, my independence over all other personal considerations?

I couldn't settle on the flight. My mind raced, unfocused, jumping from thoughts of domestic heartache to my sense of professional jeopardy and general insecurity. My mood sank lower still when, during the approach to Paris, the pilot announced that we were diverting to Frankfurt because of an electrical storm.

They put me on a bus to complete my journey, which took twelve hours. Heaping humiliation on indignity, they also lost my luggage. At 1 a.m., I was deposited on the kerb outside Gare du Nord. By this stage, my spirits were as dark and foul as the streets around the station. I was at perhaps my lowest point as an adult – reeling from the realisation of how everything in life can be blown off course with no prior warning.

I faced immediate pressure from my brothers to return to Abidjan. They advised me that staying in exile in France would make it look like I had something to hide. At the same time, many of my former cabinet colleagues were in detention. However, my confidence in my ability to get a fair hearing if I was accused of anything was low to non-existent.

Members of my former team also urged me to come back. When the mutiny started, my assistant Mylene had walked through the night to guard my office, to stop any attempt at looting. She had personally kept vigil. I've never forgotten her incredible courage and commitment in a moment that bound us together. She's now head of my cabinet.

I decided to return, though I needed to prepare properly before-hand. I went to see a friend of mine, a human rights lawyer. She gave me some advice which ranged from the mildly alarming to the downright terrifying: I should make sure my will was up to date. I should go to my doctor and request some sleeping pills. And it would be a good idea to pose for a photo session without clothes to document my physical appearance before leaving. These images would be needed for any future legal claim in the event of me being physically tortured, she said. I did everything she recom-mended.

My nerves were jangling when my phone rang as I walked to the plane to fly back to Abidjan. It was Charles Josselin, the French minister for cooperation with French-speaking countries. 'I'm call-ing to tell you that we consider you returning to be unwise,' he said.

Many of my friends and Annette felt the same way. I told Josselin that I knew I had no guarantees, and that I was the only minister returning voluntarily. He asked if I had spoken to anyone in the army, which I hadn't.

After the call, he must have alerted the French ambassador in Abidjan, who came to meet me at the international airport as I landed. The sight of him was reassuring. I said to myself that at least I would be able to leave the airport. I wouldn't be arrested immediately.

My sister was there too, as was my personal bodyguard. I walked past a soldier wearing a bandana, a machine gun slung across his shoulder. He had been posted at the bottom of the stairs leading off the plane. He recognised me and appeared friendly.

'Why did you come back?' he said to me. 'They're going to kill you.'

My father had always encouraged me to try to project strength in situations of high personal anxiety. I had been thinking of his words as the plane dipped to land. By acting strong, you override your own internal fears. And by appearing confident others are not tempted to take advantage of your weakness.

'So, where's the general?' I replied.

The soldier thought for a second. The army had sought to re-instil some discipline in the days after the coup, which had sparked car-jackings and lootings. But the chain of command was still in flux and the upheaval offered opportunities for the enterprising.

'I'll take you there,' he said.

He jumped in the car with us, and we headed to the Akouédo army barracks in Abidjan. There were groups of soldiers outside. Everyone seemed fairly relaxed, considering there were constant rumours that President Chirac would order French troops stationed in Ivory Coast to reinstate Bédié under a secret defence treaty between the countries.

One of the rebels saluted me. Some others began applauding. 'Maybe this is going to be okay,' I thought to myself. At the very least, no one had justified my fear of being hit across the face. Everything other than that was a win at this stage. I asked whether the general was on the premises. They said they didn't know but they would escort me inside. All personnel had taken off their insignia, meaning it was impossible to know their rank.

I was shown to a waiting-room where I sat until I was called for a meeting in a ground-floor office. A man introduced himself as General Mathias Doué. Tall, bespectacled and athletic-looking, he thrust out a hand and shook mine firmly. He seemed to mean business, not harm.

'I respect the fact you came back to face us,' he said tersely.

I felt the knot in my stomach unwind slightly. The spectre of being taken to a military detention centre retreated from the foreground of my mind.

'Many of your colleagues have fled. Others are in prison. I can't guarantee what is going to happen to you, but I will make sure you're treated with dignity,' he added.

If I waited, General Guéï would receive me in due course, he said.

Guéï was a wholly unimpressive character. He was neither the brightest, nor the most physically commanding, of the army top brass. Short and with stuttered speech, I suspect he had spent his life being underestimated. He was cunning in the Machiavellian sense, never the smartest person in the room, but much smarter than everyone thought he was.

He had been linked to a possible coup plot back in 1995. President Bédié had brought him into government as a result, as a way of buying his loyalty and keeping him close. Most government colleagues viewed him as toxic and shunned him as a result.

I'd always been wary but courteous when we worked together. As sports minister, he'd come to me to discuss the new Olympic stadium project. That certainly helped when seeing him face-to-face now, with our power roles entirely reversed.

Guéï told me had been forced to take over to restore order; that Bédié had lost control. He spent several minutes justifying his decision to dissolve all the country's institutions and name himself president. He was going to take a broom to the country and clean it up, he said.

I didn't sense any personal animosity from him. He also spent a long time explaining how he revered President Houphouët, who had sponsored him as a young man and sent him to military school in France. He digressed briefly and bizarrely to accuse me of 'destroying his house' – a reference to Houphouët's residence which our government had turned into a museum. He also chastised me for becoming a minister ahead of my older brother. I had failed to respect my elder – a sin in Ivorian and African culture. If these were his only complaints, they seemed like ones I could handle.

He ended by saying he wanted me to resign from my role as head of the bureau, which I said I would do. Several days later I handed over my files in front of the television cameras to my military designated successor, Seydou Diarra.

The meeting wrapped up with me asking what I should do.

'Go to your home and we'll call for you in a few days,' Guéï replied.

Driving home after this first meeting, it struck me how little had outwardly changed in Abidjan. There were slightly more soldiers on the streets, but otherwise people were out, travelling to and from work, drinking in roadside bars, hawking their wares on the pavements.

I returned to my house thinking nothing was the same for me. For several nights I barely slept. Every creak would send my pulse racing. I locked everything up, windows and doors, keeping a revolver within arm's reach of my bed just in case. I felt incredibly vulnerable. I knew that a mere accusation, through spite or calculation, a vendetta or power grab, could be enough to see me arrested. Guéï might mean me no malice, but what about the others around him?

My second meeting took place three or four days later, at the same table in his office at the army headquarters. Guéï was dressed again in army fatigues.

He thanked me for handing over the bureau. And he said his men had investigated me and recognised me as a patriot. 'Someone like you would be welcome in the new government team,' he added. 'I'd like to offer you the position of secretary-general to the president.'

I'd been prepared for a job offer, but not one of the most important positions in the country – one that would see me serve as Guéï's chief aide. I had already rehearsed what I planned to say.

'I'm extremely honoured by the offer,' I said. 'But I'm afraid I won't be able to accept. I don't want to work for a military regime.'

He stared at me for a second or two, blinking. I don't think the thought had crossed his mind that I would turn down his invitation. After what seemed like an eternity, he nodded slowly and got to his feet.

'Okay, you can go,' he said.

I attempted to soften the refusal. I said I had nothing against generals becoming presidents in principle. In fact, history had demonstrated that military men often made excellent leaders. One only need look at the examples of Charles de Gaulle in France or Ulysses S. Grant and Dwight D. Eisenhower in the United States. But if they wanted power, I was convinced they needed to stand in elections. I praised Guéï for his stated aim of holding polls quickly and returning the country to civilian rule.

Working for him would have felt like a fundamental betrayal of my values. Years later, Keki Dadiseth, a successful Indian businessman, told me he had an elegant response to people when they put him under pressure to compromise in ways that made him uncomfortable: 'I have to live with myself. You don't,' he'd say.

Beyond my lack of personal esteem for Guéï, the prospect of working for a man who could fire me on a whim and have me locked up, or worse, held no appeal. If I disagreed with Bédié, I could always resign, as I had threatened to do. He was accountable to parliament, to voters. I had some leverage and the rule of law to back me up. Guéï could have me shot.

Without institutions, without laws – the guardrails of democratic life – human existence returns to its most primitive form, an unpredictable fight for survival in which might is right. The longer I stayed in Abidjan, the less safe I felt, and the more I heard about people being abducted and disappearing.

I was also called in for a meeting by Mr Alassane Ouattara, who although he played no formal role any more, had returned to Côte d'Ivoire after the coup. He had welcomed the coup in his official statements. I was asked to meet with him I believe on 11 January 2000 and asked to come with my two older brothers, Daouda and Aziz. Our conversation did not go well and we could not see eye to eye on things.

Around a fortnight after the coup, I was driving home when four or five soldiers in a pick-up truck passed me at speed. One of them riding in the back must have recognised me at the wheel because they braked abruptly, and then reversed the truck across the road, blocking my route.

I felt every muscle in my back tense and my jaw clench. This is how it ends, I thought. This was the sort of scene I'd imagined many times during my sleepless nights.

They jumped down onto the road and started running towards me, their guns slung across their shoulders. They were young men, kids really, either drunk or high. As soon as they reached my car, they started banging on the roof.

'Thiam! Thiam! You're with us! With the general!' they shouted.

They'd obviously heard rumours that I had joined the government.

I wound the window down, almost too tense to turn my head to look at them.

'Thank you, thank you,' I said. I laughed hollowly. 'Vive le général! Thank you.'

Once they'd left, I struggled to turn the key in the ignition. Ten minutes later I was still shaking. The jolt of adrenaline, then the crash, rendered me barely able to drive home. I can't carry on like this, I thought. Never again.

My plan had always been to stick around for a few weeks. My lawyer friend had advised that when the time came to leave, I should buy a return ticket and say I was travelling to Europe to see my family.

I'd been offered another job, as advisor to the infrastructure minister Amadou Gon Coulibaly. I went to see him, telling him that I was minded to take the position, but that I needed to discuss it with my wife who, I added, was going out of her mind with worry. He called General Guéï and suggested that I be authorised to leave the country.

As I walked up to the plane a day later, my bodyguard turned and said to me softly: 'Boss, I know you're not coming back.'

I felt a lump in my throat. We'd spent so many hours together that he knew exactly how to read me.

'Shh,' I said. 'You'll get us both killed.'

The step onto the stairs of the plane would be my last one on Ivorian soil for twenty-three years. A year later elections were held, won by long-time opposition leader Laurent Gbagbo. Shortly after that, Guéï was assassinated, gunned down in his home.

Within three years, the country was plunged into civil war, ripped apart by tribal and religious tensions, cleaved in two along a faultline between the Muslim-majority north and the Christian-majority south.

I brought few possessions back with me to Paris so as not to arouse suspicion about my departure. I asked that the staff at the DCGTx agency send me my leaving present. It was a ladder made by the Dogon people of Mali, a coarse but beautiful forked tree-branch with notches carved into it for steps. It would have been used by farmers to access the upper level of their granaries. When mounted, it is sculptural in form, appearing both rugged and elegant, with the shiny, worn-down edges of its steps a reminder of the years of hard labour it had witnessed. To me, the ladder represents self-reliance, as well as the value of work. Receiving it was a cherished moment in what was then one of the lowest points of my life. I've always kept it with me since, installing it in each of my offices.

'Your destiny, boss, is to keep climbing,' my chief of staff said as he handed it over at my leaving party.

Chapter 4

London Calling

'They'd never accept you.'

I was at a meeting in one of the towers of La Défense business district in western Paris, in a room high enough to be able to see the boundary between the city's sprawl and the surrounding farmland. It was a typical executive office: all glass, aluminium, and neutral carpets. A senior manager of one of France's biggest corporations was in the process of explaining to me why he couldn't hire me. My interlocutor was superficially pained, the look in his eyes apologetic yet insincere.

'With your background and experience, and the sort of position you're interested in, we'd want to hire you to be a divisional head,' he told me. 'But I can't put you in charge of 10,000 Europeans.' He meant white people. 'They'd never accept you.'

The meeting was one of many I attended around this time, in the first years of the new millennium. Months earlier as a government minister I had been talking to the US Treasury Secretary or helping put together financing that impacted millions of lives. But now, in my early forties, I was experiencing the same spirit-crushing sensation I had felt when job-hunting after graduation.

The meeting in La Défense had been organised through my old dean at the Ecole des Mines, who had put me in contact with an alumnus of the school several years my senior. The executive's argument was a devastating indictment of his fellow French citizens, whom he viewed as too ignorant and too racist to accept a black boss. Even if he sincerely believed this, he was in a position to change their perceptions. He was hiding behind their prejudices and lacked the courage to challenge them.

He showed me out, with the relieved look of a man leaving the dentists after a successful tooth extraction. He said he would have a think and get back to me. He never took a call afterwards when I followed up, nor replied to any of my messages.

Returning to Paris after the coup had been unsettling. Having lived in fear of my life for several weeks, I was ecstatic to see my wife and children. I promised myself I would never put anything before them again, no matter how important, until our children were adults and able to look after themselves. I was the main wage-earner in our family, and I had put all of them at risk.

I remember going for a massage soon after arriving in Paris because I was having back problems. The masseuse began working on my shoulders, then stopped suddenly. 'Have you had a shock recently?' she enquired. She said she'd never felt anyone so tense. My back, she informed me, was so knotted it was as if I had experienced a near-death experience. She said she had counted thirty-two knots in the same area. I couldn't even begin to explain.

My priority was finding a new job and ensuring my first ever period of unemployment was as short as possible. One of my biggest challenges was explaining to many of the people I met was why I needed to find a job. A former African minister – especially one who had been in charge of privatisations and infrastructure development – would never normally need to work again, according to their logic. I found it amazing how casually even senior Western officials assumed that all African ministers were corrupt.

During that time, I received a job offer from Nigel Morris, co-founder and then CEO of Capital One, a financial services group, to work as global head of strategy. To this day, I am grateful to him because this did so much for my self-confidence. The company, however, was based in Charlotte, North Carolina. Flattering and tempting though the offer was, I had doubts about how well I would do as a black francophone manager in the higher echelons of a Fortune 500 company in the American South.

I asked for help from a business school classmate, who had reached a senior position in what was then one of the leading recruitment firms in the world. He told me the following:

He began sending my CV out, but changing my name to one that would lead people to believe I was white. Every time he got an excited call back, saying: 'He looks great: Ginette school, Polytechnique, Ecole des Mines, INSEAD MBA, McKinsey … When can we see him?'

He would then tell them that I was black and African. The response invariably would be: 'Well, we could not hire him.' Period. Blatant, naked discrimination.

My name was a problem, he told me bluntly. Moreover, French companies were not interested in my African experience. It was as if the last six years of my career, which were the most interesting for me personally, counted for nothing.

It had been fourteen years since I graduated from Ecole des Mines and I again struggled to find a job with a French company. I imagined that attitudes had changed since then, that the country was opening up; was more prepared to embrace diversity. On the evidence of my job-hunting, little had changed.

Around 2002, I remember going to the annual meeting of the MEDEF business group in Jouy-en-Josas, southwest of Paris, to listen to Claude Bébéar, the founder of insurance giant AXA. He told the conference hall of 2,000 business leaders that France had a problem with diversity and that there too many white faces in the room. Bébéar was then one of the most admired business people in France. Still, the audience booed him vigorously.

I went to shake his hand afterwards and congratulate him for what he had had the courage to say. There is a level of denial about racism in some of the French elite circles which is simply mind-boggling.

Fortunately, McKinsey were again incredibly supportive. They offered to take me back in their Paris office, this time as a partner. I accepted out of a sense of loyalty, and because the idea of a stable job and a comfortable salary seemed too good to be true in the circumstances.

But it was clear to me very quickly that the company had changed in the six years I had been away, growing from a very small – we were 1,000 worldwide when I joined – exclusive advisory firm to a vast corporation. And it no longer provided the thrill it once had.

In March 2002, after two years at McKinsey and numerous disappointments, I received a call from a different recruiter. He had a mandate from the CEO of a large British insurance company. They were looking for a new executive with European experience and were expressly interested in making the management board more 'international'. Did I want to know more?

'I would,' I replied. 'But I have to be frank with you: I'm fed up with being the diversity candidate on the longlist and then being eliminated. If I don't have a real chance of getting the position, I'd rather not bother.'

'That's not the case,' said the recruiter. 'The search is being led by the CEO and they're open to different profiles.'

'Okay, but can I suggest you call the CEO first? Tell him I'm 6′ 4″, black and francophone, and that I'm only interested in travelling to London if I'm going to be seriously considered.'

He agreed to make the call. The next day, he rang back.

'The CEO wants to meet you.'

I travelled to London for my first encounter with Richard Harvey, the CEO of Aviva, Britain's biggest insurance firm at the time. He welcomed me to head office in the heart of the City, cutting a tall, elegant, and benevolent figure.

His first words to me still resonate in my ears because they were such a relief after everything I had been through. I knew I was in the presence of a good, decent man: 'So you're the one who thinks I'm a racist?' he said with a wry smile. He was a vision of slightly reserved, witty Britishness.

'I'm sorry. I mean, I didn't mean it like that,' I stuttered, taken slightly off-guard. 'But with my experiences recently, it's a reasonable assumption to make.'

It felt like a promising start. His icebreaker was smart, dealing with the potentially awkward race issue with humour. He acknowledged my concerns while making it clear that they were unnecessary. We spoke briefly about racism in France, before getting down to business.

The conversation was meant to last forty-five minutes. After this time Richard's PA kept coming into the room to interrupt us, reminding him of his scheduled meetings, which he delayed or cancelled. We spent two hours talking together about the role. He wanted a new director of strategy.

The British insurance market had been consolidating fast over the previous five years. Aviva had been created by the merger, two years prior, of regional English insurance firm Norwich Union, which dominated the group, and fellow British insurer CGU. CGU was itself the result of a merger between London-based Commercial Union and Scotland's General Accident in 1998.

On top of all of this, Norwich Union and CGU had been on acquisition sprees across continental Europe before they merged. They owned a portfolio of businesses which were often leaders in their markets. Richard's priority as CEO was integrating and streamlining this vast network of companies.

I left Richard's office feeling for the first time in my various European experiences relatively confident about my chances, even though I knew one of my blue-eyed, blond-haired McKinsey colleagues was interviewing for the same position. I had a track record in financial services and had worked recently on the restructuring of a major French company. Richard and I hit it off on a personal level and I liked his manner and style.

The next day he did something quite unusual for such a recruitment process: he wrote me a letter saying that he hoped I would be offered the job and that I would accept it. He confessed later that he felt I needed reassurance that I would be treated fairly after so many bad experiences. He also arranged for me to meet the other members of the executive committee.

After a few weeks, they formally offered me the job at the end of April 2002. But with my confidence shaken by the coup and its aftermath, I hesitated for several months.

Britain was unfamiliar, outside of my usual references. I was at home in Ivory Coast, a near-native in France and an insider in the United States. London seemed culturally foreign. I was warned several times by French people that Britain was just as racist, but that people were simply more polite and hid it better. These non-impartial counsellors suggested I'd last six months before wanting to return to Paris.

I also knew, after my time working in New York, that the language would be a barrier. I felt like debate, persuasion and humour were such key parts of how I operated. Not knowing the culture was one thing. Not commanding the language in a boardroom was like running in sand when the others were on an athletics track.

We went to Mexico for a family holiday that summer and I spent every evening talking over my decision with Annette. She had always struggled in France. Despite having a job at a law firm and teaching at Sciences Po university, she felt opportunities were hard to come by in France for non-whites. The frequent and unexpected hostility encountered during daily life in Paris also ground her down. She encouraged me to make the leap back to the English-speaking business world.

'Look at what your friends are doing. You don't even get approached for jobs in France!' she told me one evening. 'How are you ever going to get a position that meets your expectations and abilities? Look at where your classmates are and where you are in your career. It's just not going to happen.'

Events around this time gave us an additional reason to move. Far-right leader Jean-Marie Le Pen made it to the second round of the French presidential elections for the first time, in a victory for racists everywhere. Jacques Chirac ended up being elected for a second term, but it was a shocking wake-up call.

Aviva were patient as they waited for me to decide, but I was finally informed that I needed to 'shit or get off the potty' by the HR director – an introduction to the sort of idiomatic British English which I would grow to love. I agreed with Annette that I would take the job and move to London first on my own. She would follow with the children in six months if all went well. I hedged my bets.

I soon realised that my caution about Britain and Aviva had been entirely unnecessary. Aviva felt like a breath of fresh air. My colour didn't seem like an issue for the first time during my professional life in Europe. In fact, they seemed to be delighted, proud even, to have appointed their first black senior executive. For the first time, I was made to feel that the fact that I looked different was a plus, an asset, not something to be hidden or tolerated.

Many of my immediate colleagues all seemed very 'establishment' – having come through Harrow, Oxbridge, or the British army – but they contained some surprises. One of them, pink-faced and outwardly as British as pork pies, was the son of two missionaries who had grown up in Papua New Guinea. He'd only learned English at the age of nine. Richard was a self-described 'grammar school boy' who went on to the University of Manchester, before spending much of his career in New Zealand. The firm were also flexible and family-focused in a way I found endearing. They had no problem with me taking a Eurostar every Friday afternoon to Paris and working from the train. On a normal day, even top managers left the office at around 6 p.m., which was a revelation to me.

Richard had me installed in a corner office next to him on the executive floor, twenty-three floors up, which was a restricted area with magnificent views over St Paul's Cathedral and all of west London. I could see the green of Hyde Park from my windows.

In one of our first meetings Richard told me that he wanted a fresh pair of eyes to look over the business. Could I meet as many people as possible, do some thinking and come back in three months with some ideas about what he should do next?

In the meantime, I was expected to run the weekly executive committee meetings, manage the IT department, which was under my responsibility, and continue to work on bringing the companies together after the merger.

The more time I spent with Richard, the more I admired him. Not just for his brilliant mind and his work ethic, but for his manner of dealing with people. Deeply religious and charming in an understated way, he had an art of making difficult decisions seem easy. In moments of high tension, I never saw him get angry. At his most confrontational, faced with the worst dysfunctions or underperformance, he would simply say 'I'm disappointed', before outlining how and why he felt let down.

The approach reminded me of my mother and how we used to dread her uttering those words. I adopted the tactic with my own children and employees, finding it a remarkably effective way of signalling your displeasure without being confrontational. Richard used to say that every manager could reprimand people or pass on negative feedback, but you needed to have earned the right to do so first.

His family included six children, two adopted, which lent balance to his life and priorities. He would often remind me, whenever I took my role too seriously or appeared obsessive about a task, that it was 'only a job'. It was the first time in my professional life that my boss, rather than driving me constantly harder, seemed to take a personal interest in my well-being.

And he was scrupulously honest, to the point where some colleagues thought he was naïve. Whereas other people might obfuscate or tell half-truths in meetings, Richard would be candid and transparent. In each of these ways, he earned my respect – becoming in the process the only person I have considered a professional mentor. Great managers have great human qualities.

In spring 2003, a few months after joining, I had finished my review of the business and organised a presentation to Richard. He liked everything to be extremely succinct. He insisted on something he called 'SOAP' whenever someone presented to the board: Summary on a Page. He viewed long documents and impenetrable detail as signs of intellectual weakness. Managers who cheated by using a small typeface for their single-page summaries fooled nobody.

My big idea was remarkably simple: Aviva should buy Prudential, its biggest and oldest rival in the UK. The industry was heading for more consolidation and, once the cost-cutting had been completed, future profitability would be driven by growth. The only markets where growth would be available on a sufficient scale were in Asia. Prudential was much better established and positioned in emerging markets in the East than Aviva.

Richard was sceptical.

'We make more money in Liverpool than Prudential does in the whole of Asia,' he countered.

At the time, Prudential was making something like £60 million in Asia while Aviva was making around £500 million in profits in the UK. Looking at this in a static way, Richard was right.

'But it's about growth,' I said. 'In twenty years, that £500 million in the UK will still be 500 million. In Asia you'll be making billions,' I argued.

We had a discussion, going back-and-forth with arguments.

I spent the next three years trying to make him see the logic, finally making headway in 2006 when we began talks about a friendly takeover. It faced serious internal opposition from other board members in Aviva, including the then CFO (chief financial officer) Andrew Moss, who did not believe in Asian markets.

The talks leaked to the media at the wrong time, Prudential ended up rejecting our offer, and Richard backed away after a meeting with our bankers. I was chastened, but undeterred.

Richard also put me in charge of a cursed IT project called 'the Global Finance Transformation Programme', with a budget over £200 million and hundreds of consultants. It was meant to integrate twenty-three different accounting systems around the world to prepare Aviva for the new IFRS accounting rules, which were looming in 2004. The company had been burning tens of millions of pounds every year on the delayed project, costing several finance directors their jobs.

One rugby-loving colleague of mine said I had been given the 'hospital pass of the century' – another amusing expression I noted for future use. (I should add that I didn't always master 'Britishisms'. When I spoke to a room of journalists about 'taking things with a finger of salt', instead of a pinch, some of them looked back at me with blank bemusement.) I told Richard I knew how important the project was and, also, how much everyone despised it. At a time when the company was cutting jobs and costs, everyone knew it was splurging on expensive IT and management consultants who were failing to deliver. The task could have buried my career, but instead it made my name internally.

Part of the problem was that the demands and specifications of the IT system were constantly changing. Business heads kept requesting new functionalities, which extended the scope of the software. Lots of ideas – including new datasets or creating visualisation tools, for example – were useful but highly disruptive.

I explained to the team that not every good idea was desirable and not everything desirable needed to be done. My priority was freezing the design, then focusing on implementation. The project needed discipline and rigour. I was helped in that task by an excellent project director, David Paige. Within six months, we were on track for completion, and I actually learned an enormous amount about insurance accounting, which would help me later.

My personal life in London had started slowly. But after several months of travelling back and forth to Paris, the boys, then aged eight and six, said they wanted us all to move to London together. I'd found a nice home in Knightsbridge and felt confident enough to bring Annette and the children over. The move was a commitment to putting down roots.

We found great schools for the kids. My eldest son, Bilal, had by this time been diagnosed with Central Auditory Processing Disorder (CAPD). It's a rare condition that affects how verbal commands and information are interpreted. It makes it difficult to interpret spoken instructions and renders rowdy environments such as classrooms or play areas confusing spaces of white noise. Children with CAPD need to be taught differently to other kids, emphasising visual learning instead of auditive teaching.

It's often hard to detect, meaning many children have reached the age of nine or ten by the time they are identified. Up until that point, they are often treated like idiots by their teachers, as Bilal was at his expensive private school in Paris. The principal had asked us to withdraw him because his marks were going to bring down the average of his school year.

Through Bilal's experiences, I encountered a whole range of extraordinary children who taught me so much about neurodiversity. They opened my eyes to the complexities of human development and how we often think about achievement and education in the wrong way. It changed how I recruited people too.

I marvelled at the positive reinforcement in my boys' schools and the efforts made to promote their self-esteem. They had a marking system with two columns, one for achievement and one for effort. I would tell the boys that the achievement score alone was often simply a reflection of a pupil's natural endowment. What I was interested in was their effort, whether they had given it their best shot. That reflected character, which is a much better indicator of future success and fulfilment.

French schools would benefit from such changes. In French primary schools, appraisals for children's work often still start at zero and then descend, with each mistake counted. A score of nought is therefore the highest any pupil can achieve.

When I was at Polytechnique, I had an average of 8/20, even though I was performing well and working close to my maximum capacity. When some of my peers applied for places on postgraduate courses at US universities, they had to send an accompanying letter to explain why their marks looked so low. A score of 8/20 would make you a failure in the US system.

I suspect the confidence-sapping education system is at least part of the explanation for the famously prickly French temperament.

As we settled into London, we'd spend weekends as a family together in Hyde Park, sometimes socialising with colleagues. The migration to the UK of many ambitious French graduates had also begun. I reconnected with friends from Polytechnique who had moved there. I also watched games at my beloved Arsenal Football Club.

It's a cliché, but the only thing I struggled with was the food, which was a pale imitation of what I'd become accustomed to in Paris. But what Britain lacked in fine restaurants – I should add that the gap between Paris and London has since narrowed – it more than compensated for in other ways.

*   *   *

In 2003, less than a year after I moved over, I received a call from an official in Downing Street saying that he wanted to come to see me. It was Ambassador Myles Wickstead. The then prime minister Tony Blair was putting together a 'Commission for Africa', he told me. The idea was to place development and debt relief at the heart of his agenda for the Group of Eight (G8) summit of world leaders in Gleneagles in Scotland, which was scheduled for 2005. His team was interested in appointing me to the commission, along with people like Meles Zenawi, the outstanding prime minister of Ethiopia, Kofi Annan, and other prominent African leaders.

How had they found me? I marvelled at their ingenuity. The last UK official I'd spoken to had been the British ambassador to Abidjan in 1999, before the coup. I had no public profile in London to speak of and had not sought out any institutional contacts. Yet someone, somewhere had identified and located me. It's a tribute to the 'soft power' of Britain.

I liked the idea of the commission. Firstly, it would mean working with other Africans. Secondly, Blair was promising to take an active personal interest. Relations with Africa were being given the same level of importance as those usually reserved for the United States or China.

On top of this, there seemed a genuine openness to new ideas. As Blair said when he announced it in February 2004, he wanted to know: 'What has worked, what has not worked, and what more can and should be done.'

My main question each time I was offered this sort of position was whether I felt passionately about the subject. Would I feel sufficiently enthusiastic to find the time and make the effort required in parallel to my busy corporate life? If not, I felt I would be taking a spot from someone else who might contribute more effectively. I was swayed by the fact that Blair wanted to put debt relief at the heart of our work. I knew there was a chance the commission might turn out to be another 'talking shop', but it was one that held out the possibility of selling some serious ideas to G8 leaders at the summit in July.

In the end, Blair and the Chancellor of the Exchequer, Gordon Brown, sat in on all of our meetings, a tribute to their engagement. I've taken part in similar exercises since and never experienced the same level of commitment. The final report was also thorough and excellent, coordinated by leading academic and fellow mathematician Nick Stern, who was then working at the Treasury.

I insisted we have a workstream on peace and security, even threatening to resign my role unless it was included. As I explained to everyone, I was working in London because my country was being ripped apart by civil war. There was no point talking about infrastructure and economic growth until you have peace and security, the pre-conditions to any nation's development.

I also argued forcefully for debt relief, an issue I felt passionately about. I'd seen the ravages caused by an unsustainable debt burden, which deprived millions of people of essential services. I'd studied in a state high school in Abidjan that lacked enough chairs for every pupil. I'd seen the effects of not having enough classrooms for a population growing at nearly 4 per cent a year. I'd had to explain to government employees why they wouldn't receive their salaries.

The G8 Gleneagles summit saw the cancellation of debts worth more than $100 billion, mostly owed to international organisations such as the IMF and World Bank – a huge contribution to poverty alleviation in Africa over the next ten years. It also saw the G8 nations commit to increasing their annual development aid by $50 billion a year. Like most pledges, it never reached the target, but they did increase spending by around $30 billion, according to the charity Oxfam.

I admired Blair and Brown for succeeding in creating momentum and public pressure for action with their creative approach to politics and diplomacy, together with Bob Geldof, who was a driving force behind this effort. Blair and Brown enlisted people outside of politics from civil society, like me, but also from the arts: Bono and Sir Paul McCartney played to a huge crowd in Hyde Park for a 'Live 8' concert on the eve of the summit with a simple message: 'Make Poverty History'.

Life in London felt rich, fresh and full of opportunity. Five years earlier I had been unemployed in Paris. I was now helping the British government, continuing to work on development in Africa, while being paid well in a stimulating day job.

At Aviva, I moved on from my position as strategy director to become managing director of the company's international unit, which comprised a range of disparate businesses from the United States to Spain, to many Eastern European countries. Richard Harvey told me that he planned to create a new single European division, which would be roughly half the company and include big markets such as France, the Netherlands and Germany. I had been earmarked for the role, he said. I suspected he was priming me for the CEO job.

In fact, the move created the first crack in our relationship. Out of fifteen markets that I would have responsibility for in Europe, the country heads in fourteen of them expressed their support. The only one who objected? The head of ... France. He believed having me as CEO would be 'an insult to him, to his company and his country', he told my predecessor in the role, who passed on the remark to the CEO, Richard Harvey, my boss.

An insult to France? Seriously? I had proved myself inside the company, at headquarters, for the past four years. I'd been to his country's top universities. He clearly had serious misconceptions about the importance of his business to the nation. But more importantly it was impossible to imagine him saying this if I had been white, or European. I physically shook with anger when I heard it.

I complained to Richard. I said it was crazy. Although I was always reluctant to raise it as an issue, I said this smacked of racism.

He needed to take a stand. Instead, he said he needed a few months to smooth things over with the French executive. Although I always admired Richard's consensual manner, I believed this was a moment that called for firmness.

Around the same time, a headhunter working for Lloyd's of London, the insurance company, approached me about becoming their CEO. They were a much smaller operation but hugely prestigious. Everybody in the world has heard of Lloyd's of London and its insurance contracts. The idea was appealing. Annette encouraged me to take it, seeing it as an opportunity to become the first black CEO in Britain. Both of us marvelled at how doors seemed to keep opening in the highest echelons of the City of London.

I did some interviews, made the shortlist, and was selected from the final three candidates. I accepted the job and went to see Richard in his office.

'You can't do this,' he said. He was upset and hurt. 'I brought you to this country, I've always backed you. I need you to stay to drive the company forward.'

He then told me something he hadn't planned on revealing. He was planning to step down the year after. The implication was that the CEO job would be opening, and I would have a shot at it.

I did feel indebted to him. He'd taken a chance on me, which many others had refused to do. Even though I knew the Aviva CEO job was not in his gift – the board would lead the search – I agreed to stay on. I called the Lloyd's chairman, Lord Levene, and reversed my decision. He didn't speak to me for years afterwards.

But when Richard did step down twelve months later, I didn't even get an interview. By this stage, I was head of Europe, managing operations in France and fourteen other European countries. I was responsible for half the company's revenues. I'd overseen major acquisitions in Italy, Spain and Turkey. Sales were up 16 per cent. But I didn't even make the longlist of candidates. It was a huge shock.

I went to see Richard and reminded him of what he'd told me, how I'd turned down the chance to be CEO of Lloyd's to stay at Aviva. 'There's no way I can get this board to appoint you,' he told me. There was a hint of shame in his eyes. He knew the reasons but didn't elaborate. I didn't feel there was any point in pressing further.

My attachment to the company, the thread of loyalty snapped internally. When they appointed finance director Andrew Moss to the top job, a man I didn't believe should be my boss, I knew it was time to move on. I no longer trusted them.

At about the same time, the CEO of Prudential came knocking. Mark Tucker became the second hugely influential figure for my career in the City. In character, he couldn't have been more different. If Richard was slightly reserved and emotionally buttoned up, Mark was garrulous and sometimes abrasive, a man given to slapping you on the shoulder with a loud guffaw. He was physically imposing and his reputation on the football pitch was fearsome.

'They're idiots to pass you over for the CEO job, come work for Prudential,' he told me at the start of a charm offensive that would take place over many weeks of secret meetings.

We couldn't be seen together, so he would invite me to a flat in Belgravia that was owned by his parents-in-law. I knew Mark already from the industry. He had helped build up Prudential in Asia, which was the reason I wanted Aviva to buy the company in the first place. He'd been brought back in as CEO in 2005 to pull the company out of a decline, a task he had set about with his customary vigour.

We were very much aligned in our way of thinking, in our interest in Asia, as well as our view that traditional insurance in Western Europe was a low-return, low-growth business. The profits were in capital-light new products, such as health insurance, as well as life insurance, which were in high demand among the emerging middle classes of Asia.

He offered me the CFO job. I said I would take it, providing it gave me a clear path to the CEO position. Mark said he planned to step down in a couple of years which would give me time to prove myself. Compared to Aviva, he assured me that Prudential was much more international-minded and would be more open to appointing an outsider as CEO. As Mark reminded me, he was South African and Jewish.

Richard was hurt and felt betrayed by the news of my departure. Andrew Moss was dismissive and rude when I informed him: we had a heated meeting in which he accused me of trying to deliberately undermine him. I said I understood it was difficult but suggested we get together in a few months once the dust had settled.

'I don't think so,' he replied. He gave me five minutes to empty my desk and leave the building.

I left animated by a strong desire to take revenge. A lot of my subsequent work at Prudential was intended to cause as much pain as possible to Aviva. The flip side of being a loyal person is that I feel betrayals very deeply.

Chapter 5

The Man from 'The Pru'

M oving to 'The Pru', as it is known in the UK, was one of my better decisions. Within a year, in March 2009, I was named as CEO. The media and the public commentary predictably focused on my skin colour. *The Times* said I had 'created history by becoming the first black chief executive of a FTSE 100 company'. The *Daily Mail, Guardian*, and almost all other media ran headlines that included the words 'first black boss'.[1] It was understandable; I was a novelty and therefore news.

But I'll be honest: in what was the highest point of my business career, it made me feel conflicted and uncomfortable. Of course I was happy to be seen as pushing boundaries, smashing ceilings, breaking ground, or redefining the image of the City, boardrooms, Britain and much else – I was credited with an absurd list of achievements in the sometimes overwrought coverage that followed.

Yet like any other public figure whose physical appearance, nationality or other unalterable fact becomes one of their defining characteristics, I felt somewhat minimised, essentialised, reduced to the pigmentation of my skin. Of course, as a person and as an executive, I felt much more than a 'black boss'. In fact, a big part of me wanted my skin colour to be an irrelevance, whereas its significance underlined how far we still had to go to become post-racial societies.

To dwell on it felt like giving too much importance to the absurdity of race, that eighteenth-century construct of European colonial minds. I'd always struggled with the idea of being identified by something so unscientific, so imprecise, so regressive. Why should my skin colour be any more relevant than, say, my being right-handed? However well intentioned, the intense scrutiny felt like a victory for the racists.

I didn't talk about it publicly, and you'll never find a quote from me talking up my blackness or my supposed success as a role model for others. What's more, being defined simply as 'black' sat uneasily. For an African, you only become 'black' when you travel away from the continent, when you are stripped of all your other ethnic and cultural identifiers, as slaves were when they were shipped across the Atlantic.

In Africa, I have multiple identities: I'm Ivorian – Baoulé culturally through my mother, but also Senegalese and Toucouleur through my father. No one in Ivory Coast thinks of themselves primarily as black. I also viewed myself as harbouring influences from France as well as Morocco. *The Sunday Times* highlighted my supposedly 'exotic past'[2] – an unfortunate choice of language.

As so many of the anecdotes illustrate in this book, race remains such a strong social phenomenon and a collective lived experience. Racism has been a feature of my own family history, a blight in my professional life, and a personal combat. As much as I might try to wish away the divisions and awkwardness it creates, it keeps intruding.

Others pondered what my nomination said about Britain's attitudes to race and the success of the country's social model. I wasn't sure I could be held up as an example of successful integration by Britain: I came to the country as a forty-year-old who was headhunted in the financial services industry. I wasn't a kid born to low-income black parents somewhere in the UK who had won a university scholarship then worked his way up through the City.

That would be better proof of social mobility than the successful immigrant that I was.

The year before becoming CEO, in the Powerlist ranking, produced by Powerful Media, I was named as the second-most influential black person in the UK behind Sudan-born billionaire Dr Mo Ibrahim. Interestingly, three of the top four that year were born and raised in Africa and had careers before coming to the UK.

My own view was that Britain clearly still had work to do to provide improved opportunities to the children of immigrants, the sort of kids who live on housing estates that can be found a stone's throw from the City. But I felt sure that my promotion was a sign that the country, while certainly not colour-blind, was much more open, tolerant, and daring than its European peers. From my experience, Britain is decades ahead of other European nations in the way it treats its minorities in general. As I write in 2025, none of the companies on the French CAC 40 index of leading companies has had a black CEO. It's the same story in Germany and Italy.

My appointment entirely vindicated my decision to leave France after becoming frustrated by a unique combination of small-mindedness and 'good conscience' exhibited by some of the members of the country's business elite. The public reaction to my nomination in the UK was overwhelmingly positive and financial markets signalled their approval: Prudential's share price rose several per cent on the day. The announcement met with surprisingly tepid praise in some quarters, however.

Trevor Phillips, the then head of the Commission for Racial Equality (CRE), told journalists he couldn't celebrate my appointment because he didn't know the circumstances. It seemed an oddly cool reception from one of Britain's leading black voices and a noted campaigner for diversity. I wondered whether being a French-speaking foreigner, and not West Indian or an anglophone African, counted against me.

One person I would've loved to have shared the news with was my father, who had done so much to encourage me to study hard and to excel academically. He had always pushed me to venture into areas that had been previously closed off or restricted to Africans and black people. He died a few weeks before the announcement, after a long and courageous fight against cancer. Sadly, I never got to tell him that I had jumped the battlements and now led a boardroom where he would not even have been physically admitted a few decades ago.

My promotion to CEO was by no means inevitable after I joined Prudential in 2008. There was fierce internal competition, with the head of the UK business, Nick Prettejohn, seen as a very strong candidate. I took nothing for granted until Mark Tucker and chairman Harvey McGrath walked into my office to inform me at the end of a very thorough assessment process. I had been chosen just as I was putting the finishing touches to my first set of full-year results.

My time as CFO had been extraordinarily busy and Mark and I had helped steer the company through one of its most tumultuous periods. My timing when moving jobs has always been terrible, or fortunate, depending on how you look at it. When I returned to Ivory Coast, they had just pushed through a 50 per cent devaluation, the first in more than forty years. In 2003, when I joined Aviva, the Iraq War began. At Prudential, I immediately experienced a once-in-a-century financial crisis.

I've always felt temperamentally equipped to deal with stress at work. Nothing the business world can throw at you compares with your father being imprisoned, or being put under house arrest, or being stopped on the road by drunken soldiers. One thing I do not do is panic. I also arrived at Prudential mentally primed for trouble.

I'd spent six months on gardening leave between leaving Aviva and taking up my new position. I'd used the time to read a lot –

books, academic papers, and the media – as well as consult my professional contacts, including at the World Bank and the International Monetary Fund. During that period out of work, paradoxically I felt so much more in touch, more connected than during my regular working life.

It provided a lesson in how easy it is to get isolated and disconnected in the business world when you're focused on the tasks right in front of you, the day-to-day grind of meetings and deadlines – a bit like a cyclist who sees no further than his handlebars or the next corner. Unless you're looking further forward and scanning the horizon regularly, you're probably failing to interpret important signals which should guide your decision-making. When you're running a company, it is so easy to misread your environment.

My extended holiday taught me the value of time out. What became clear to me was that the US real estate market was an accident waiting to happen. The glut of lax lending to uncreditworthy households meant that many banks were holding huge liabilities that were potentially toxic and incredibly sensitive to an economic downturn.

I also investigated the role of so-called mortgage-backed securities (MBSs), which had been sold in their billions by investment bankers to investors, effectively spreading the risk of the US real estate market throughout the financial system. In August 2007, French bank BNP Paribas had announced that it had no way of valuing MBSs owned by some of its funds.

The bankers, including Credit Suisse (more of this later) had sliced and diced bundles of often poor-quality home loans and turned them into supposedly ultra-low-risk, AAA-rated investments which were purchased by pension funds, insurance companies, and asset managers but also by non-financial companies looking for higher yields with 'low risk'. The problem was that in many cases the underlying assets were so-called 'sub-prime' home loans, which were highly risky. Those were then 'wrapped' with insurance, supposedly enhancing their credit quality. Somehow the banks had chopped up garbage credit and turned it into pristine debt in a conjuring trick that fooled everyone from the regulators to the most sophisticated investors.

I'd seen before how major financial problems are sometimes hiding in plain sight. When I was at McKinsey in 2001, the Franco-Belgian utility group Suez-Tractebel had wanted to know how US rival Enron was so successful and could constantly outbid them. I couldn't work it out either and 'experts' in the field kept telling me I just didn't understand. Somehow Enron had discovered something that nobody had thought about before them: using Special Purpose Vehicles (SPVs), subsidiaries created by the parent company, which magically lowered Enron's cost of capital.

It has been my experience that when someone can't explain something to you, it's either because they're hiding something, or they don't understand it themselves, or both. Too often people doubt themselves. I just couldn't understand Enron's SPVs and why they seemed to magically create value. It didn't make sense to me. It failed the age-old common-sense test.

While on holiday in Spain in August 2007, I decided to liquidate most of my personal investments and hold cash. There were several flashing warning lights: US home sales were falling fast and trading in MBSs and the myriad of derivative instruments built on them was drying up fast. For a few weeks, my decision looked questionable as I missed out on significant gains as markets rallied. Some of my friends told me I was foolish. But the mistake many investors make is trying to sell up at the very top of the market; you have to be extraordinarily lucky to exit at the peak.

My concerns informed a major business decision that I had to be involved in and which immediately brought me into conflict with some Prudential executives. Prudential had announced to the market with great fanfare before I joined the company that it would distribute a part of what it considered excess capital to around four million policyholders, who were waiting for a windfall of several hundred pounds each. The move understandably had been very positively received.

The excess capital was from what was known as Prudential's 'inherited estate' – unclaimed money that had accumulated in the company's main with-profit investment fund, which was worth around £90 billion at the time. Prudential ran Britain's best-performing fund, which had been going for more than a hundred years. The inherited estate of £8.7 billion was money that had built up over that time and had never been distributed to policyholders. The funds were usually invested in stocks, which gave solid returns during good times, and provided a buffer and security in lean periods. It had been called upon in 2002 when markets crashed at the end of the dot-com boom.

The chief actuary at Prudential, David Belsham, came to see me and made it clear that he thought distributing the inherited estate was mistaken. Together we drew up a thirty-page memo to the board outlining why we thought drawing down Prudential's capital was not a good idea. In a major market downturn, the company and its shareholders would potentially face huge liabilities. There were multiple scenarios in which we would burn through the inherited estate. In a major financial crisis, we could face disaster: bankruptcy for our proud 160-year-old company.

I went to see Mark and hoped to convince him. He wondered if I was being overly cautious and alarmist. Together with David, we took the issue to the chairman and the rest of the board. They could see the risks and backed our view. In June 2008, we announced that the redistribution was being cancelled, causing the share price to fall.

For several months, I felt like a high-profile signing for a successful Premier League football club whose arrival sparks a string of bad results. But by September, the U-turn took on a different hue. We faced the Armageddon scenario that I had described in my memo: US homeowners in default were walking away from their properties in droves. The US government bailed out mortgage providers Fannie Mae and Freddie Mac.* Lehman Brothers imploded. The financial system went into meltdown.

From September until the end of 2008, I worked most nights until 2–3 a.m. I would go home at 11 p.m. and then work from my office there, handling US business, before getting up for the open of European markets. On one day in October, Prudential's share price dropped 16 per cent, the next day another 10 per cent.

Prudential is the oldest quoted insurance company in the UK. Since its creation in 1848, six of the ten worst intra-day trading performances for its stock took place in October 2008. I began joking that a good day in the office was when you had only one bank failure to deal with.

There were multiple times when I wondered if the company would survive. In October, there were rumours that Lloyds TSB was about to fail after its disastrous acquisition of stricken British mortgage provider HBOS the month before. Prudential held a billion euros in cash in Lloyds accounts.

I made a call to Paul Tucker, who was the number two at the Bank of England at the time. I told him I'd heard the rumours that Lloyds was about to declare bankruptcy. 'I know this has been a nightmare for the last three weeks and the worst time of our lives, but I want to make sure you are fully aware of what's at stake. If you let Lloyds fail, not only will you have a banking crisis as you already do, you'll have an insurance crisis too,' I said. 'If the Pru goes down, it's the end of the world.'

It's one thing to lose your bank savings. It's quite another to lose your pension which you've been counting on for your end-of-life

---

* The Federal National Mortgage Association (Fannie Mae) and the Federal Home Loan Mortgage Corporation (Freddie Mac) were created by Congress to provide reliable and affordable mortgage funds throughout the United States.

income. Politically and economically, it's an economic crisis of a different magnitude. Paul Tucker understood this and gave us enough time to protect our bank deposits and our capital position. In the end, the Bank of England and the British government had no choice but to step in and rescue Lloyds, along with RBS, with taxpayers' money.

Another crucial moment came in December when I had an eight-hour conference call with our US finance team and our auditors, KPMG. I began it pacing up and down in my office, and finished it at home, sometimes pleading with them, other times barking complaints. Hearing my voice raised late at night, the children wondered what was going on. The fate of the company hinged on whether KPMG would sign off on our full-year accounts.

Accounting rules can break companies, especially those with long-term business models like insurance firms. At stake was whether KPMG was going to force us to mark our US assets at market values at a time when markets were completely dysfunctional. There was no liquidity and it had become close to impossible to assign a value to a lot of our bonds, which we felt were still credit-worthy and showed no sign of failing. In the middle of a credit crisis and a generalised loss of confidence, many of our safe long-term assets – even the safest among them such as ten-year US government bonds – had dramatically lower market values. In some cases, bonds that were sound and financially safe had fallen to 20 per cent of their previous value for no reason other than fear and a lack of liquidity in the market. The price of those fixed income assets no longer reflected credit risk. It reflected panic. If we had marked these assets to market value in our results, we'd have had to raise fresh capital to cover our liabilities – but raising capital was impossible in those conditions. Without access to cash, we'd have had no choice but to declare bankruptcy.

In the end, the issue escalated all the way to the lead partner of KPMG, Guy Bainbridge. Prudential's existence and my career lay in his hands. He ended up accepting my request to not mark the assets to market. He said he would take personal responsibility for the decision. Guy is a brave and good man, and I can tell you from experience that such characters are few and far between at times of crisis. To this day, I feel indebted to him. By 11 p.m. we were saved, and I knew we would make it somehow through this hell.

As a rookie CFO, I wasn't just thrown in the deep end during the global financial crisis of 2008. I was taken on a vessel to the Mariana Trench and cast overboard. I was fortunate to have an excellent team of specialists around me who I could call on for help when needed. And what I lacked in technical accounting skills, I tried to make up for with my deep understanding of the underlying businesses and how our products worked.

One of my organising principles throughout, which I would apply rigorously as CEO during other difficult moments, was to be as transparent as possible with everyone, including staff and the markets. Traders and investors know exactly what to do when they hear good news; they will take a considered view on bad news. What they hate more than anything is uncertainty. The more information you can give them, the more rationally they will behave.

Prudential was exposed to the US real estate market through our Michigan-based subsidiary Jackson National Life. It held most of the MBSs we owned, which by 2009 were worth a fraction of their book value. The MBSs were in funds which were used to finance its variable annuity products, which were some of the most complex financial products I had ever encountered. Of all the variable annuity providers in the United States, Jackson ended up being the one that didn't blow up.

Part of the difficulty was in identifying and quantifying our exposure. I needed to rapidly understand how Jackson had hedged its positions and whether the options it had taken out would cover enough of the losses it was now exposed to. Some of my experience during my unhappy year at the World Bank would come in handy: I'd spent six months there working on options pricing models.

Once I had drilled down into the figures, I was convinced that Jackson was well insulated, and its trading strategy had been sound. There was nothing wrong with their underlying business. As we gathered the information we needed, financial markets went through wild gyrations, seemingly fired by raw emotion rather than logic. I also saw the malign influence of hedge funds at work. As a devoted capitalist, I have nothing against hedge funds, in theory. They provide liquidity in financial markets and are set up to take risks that others, such as banks and insurance companies, should not.

But their behaviour during the global financial crisis, when they acted in unison to manipulate share prices, was indefensible. I fervently believe in capitalism and free markets, but in order to work for the benefit of society they need laws, effective regulation and enforcement.

Hedge funds would sell our stock en masse while feeding rumours that Jackson was a financial blackhole with the potential to sink the company. Acting in cahoots, they had the firepower to drive the price down. Once it began falling, they'd take advantage of a panic-driven sell-off by shorting the stock and cashing in, making hundreds of millions in the process. This pattern of systematically targeting companies eventually led regulators in London and New York to ban short-selling in financial stocks, although no one was ever prosecuted.

The only answer to the manipulation was disclosure. I did presentation after presentation outlining what our exposure was to the US real estate market, Jackson's hedging positions, and our confidence that it could weather the storm. In our third-quarter results, we innovated among insurance companies by giving more than sixty pages of detailed disclosures on our holdings, warts and all. We held long, painstaking calls with investors, offering to stay on the line for as long as there were questions. It is one of my beliefs that imagination is generally worse than reality. There is little downside in being transparent. Most predicted Armageddon from us when I made those disclosures, but they were in fact very well received, and soon investors were asking all insurance companies for the disclosures we had pioneered.

Those disclosures didn't stop the rumours or the share-price pressure. We were heavily exposed to the US and Britain, the two worst-hit countries, as well as China which some commentators speculated could be the next domino to fall. Our more conservative (and much duller) French and German counterparts fared much better. At our lowest valuation, Prudential was worth just £8 billion with a share price of £1.96.

As Rudyard Kipling wrote: 'If you can keep your head when all about you are losing theirs, yours is the Earth.' I remember speaking to chairman Harvey McGrath and we discussed a management buyout of the company given the ludicrously low valuation of it. But we had no way of raising that sort of capital, unfortunately. In any crisis, cash is king. When I left Prudential as CEO seven years later, the company was worth £68 billion.

In the middle of this turmoil, Mark Tucker dropped a different sort of bombshell. He told me in late 2008 that he had changed his mind and that he wanted to step down earlier than expected. There were rumours in the press that there were tensions between us, but that was not true. He planned to be gone by June of 2009, he said. My shock was so visible that Mark joked afterwards that he'd never seen a black man go white except that day.

The company needed stability more than anything. It was still at the mercy of contagion on financial markets. I also suspected that the change was too soon for me. My understanding with Mark when I joined Prudential was that he would stay in his position long enough for me to gain the experience required to make a serious pitch for the CEO position.

'No, no, you've done a great job, you can still make it,' he assured me.

It turned out he was right. Once I was named CEO, Mark intended to spend six months handing over to me, but it soon became clear that the transition would be much shorter. It became a challenging period for both of us, despite the excellent working relationship we enjoyed. Any decision he made would be checked with me as the incoming CEO, which is unfortunately human nature in those types of situations.

I owed Mark a great deal and admired his energy and skill. We'd been through a huge amount together in a very short, intense period. Everyone who worked in the City during the global financial crisis has been scarred for life. We were no different. The bonds forged over those months are deep and long lasting.

I spent many Sundays at his house, preparing for the week ahead. We'd sometimes watch football together on Saturdays to escape the pressure – he'd invite me to watch Chelsea; I'd take him to Arsenal. Throughout our time together we'd talk for hours and hours about a company we both admired: AIA, the Asian division of US insurance behemoth AIG. Mark knew it intimately having spent years building up Prudential as a rival in Asia in the 2000s. In countries where Prudential was second largest, AIA was top, and vice versa. It was the only company to have a similar network of agents to Prudential and it had a much bigger footprint than we had in China.

When AIG was rescued by the US government at the start of the financial crisis in September 2008, Mark and I both sensed an opportunity. If the Western part of AIG was a 'basket case', the Asian business by contrast was still as strong and promising as ever. We travelled to Singapore to try to convince the Singaporean sovereign wealth fund, Temasek, to back us in a takeover of AIA.

Facing huge losses on their global investments, and fearful that Prudential itself was a ticking bomb, Temasek wouldn't support us. We tried everything to reassure them that Jackson was on a sound footing, even sending some of their executives to the US. Instead, they invested in US investment banks Merrill Lynch and Citigroup in what turned out to be catastrophic loss-making decisions. Mark and I were bitterly disappointed.

In late 2009, less than half a year into my time as CEO, I saw another opening. AIG and the US government, which owned a large swathe of the US financial sector at this point, said they were going to execute a spin-off AIA as a separate unit to raise cash.

I made a secret trip to AIG headquarters in New York to meet my counterpart Robert 'Bob' Benmosche, the latest boss in the hotseat. The company was based in a world-famous Art Deco-style skyscraper on Pine Street in Lower Manhattan, a pharaonic building of sixty-nine floors in keeping with AIG's pre-crisis status as the world's biggest insurance company. I instantly warmed to Bob, a large, warm character who had grown up running a motel with his mother and had done two war tours in Vietnam as a volunteer with the US Signal Corps. His CEO suite at the top of the building had a terrace so big we could have played golf on it, with breathtaking views over the East River. It was easy to feel like the master of the universe up there, perhaps part of the explanation for the company's overreach under Bob's predecessors.

I told him about my time in Ivory Coast, the coup, and my decision to move back to Europe. We talked through my time at Aviva and my vision for Prudential. Then I made my pitch to take over AIA, outlining how a combination with Prudential would mean the two companies would be market leaders in sixteen Asia markets. Prudential would grow AIA's business and guarantee a future for its employees.

If we could agree the right price, Bob said he would support me. He needed cash to pay down government loans, and a takeover by Prudential was a safer option than running an IPO in six months' time, when markets would still be volatile. I said I was thinking of a figure of around $35 billion.

We shook hands.

The next steps were to persuade the AIG board and the US Treasury to back me. I conducted everything in extreme secrecy, knowing that a leak could kill the deal – a decision that would come back to bite me.

I was convinced that $35 billion represented value, given the synergies between the companies. But raising that sort of capital so soon after the financial crisis was going to be challenging. I began a long series of consultations with our major institutional shareholders, including Larry Fink at BlackRock and Maurizio Lualdi at Capital International, who were both supportive. I knew many smaller shareholders would baulk. They were sitting on huge losses, and everyone was struggling for cash. I needed time to prepare the ground and my arguments.

On my way back on a Saturday, after a meeting with the AIG board in New York at the end of February 2010, news of the negotiations leaked to Mark Kleinman, a renowned business journalist at Sky News. After three months of secrecy, our cover was blown. I had a lot of explaining to do and not a lot of time before markets opened on Monday morning.

Looking back now, the leak torpedoed the deal. Our share price fell 16 per cent on Monday, which was a logical reaction: we were going to need to raise $20 billion in a rights issue which would massively dilute the value of existing shares. The amount we needed was more than the whole company was worth at that point.

Many of our small shareholders were lost from this point onwards, their imaginations set against the transaction. Psychologists call this 'cognitive priming'. It relates to how our minds are influenced by the first piece of information they receive about a topic. The news reports had made the deal sound like a terrifying mountain ascent. I had a route planned out, a phalanx of porters, and knew that the view at the top would be worth it. But getting this message through was now almost impossible.

I did a presentation on the Monday, laying out the case for the merger and the potential for growth of the combined companies. We had 250,000 insurance agents in Asia; they had 500,000. I had slides showing the forecast growth in insurance products in the decade ahead. In the end, the audience of analysts and investors appeared convinced. Lualdi, our lead shareholder at Capital Group, was overheard saying: 'It's game over. Prudential got an amazing deal.'

But many others just couldn't get past the price tag, which they wanted lowered. Or they were simply spooked by the idea of doing the biggest deal in insurance history and Britain's biggest foreign takeover at a time of such economic uncertainty. I argued that the crisis was a golden opportunity.

By May, I realised that I was going to struggle to win over the 75 per cent of shareholders which I needed to push the deal through. In an attempt to convince some of the doubters, I returned to AIG at the end of the month with a lower offer. It was a last roll of the dice, an attempt to renegotiate the price tag. Bob, who loved the deal as much as I did, agreed and signed off a price reduction from $35 billion to $30 billion: a major concession.

But when the AIG board met, they refused to renegotiate. Bob, who wasn't on the board, was asked to leave the room when they discussed it.

'It's over,' he emailed me afterwards. 'This too shall pass.'

The media coverage in the following days was brutal. The *Financial Times* quoted several shareholders saying they would push for my ousting after the 'shambles'.[3] There were question marks about my experience and temperament. The company was on the hook for gigantic legal costs and other fees. A journalist in the *Telegraph* described me as an 'incompetent fool'.[4]

The general view was that I was toast, burned after less than twelve months in the job, an Icarus figure who had aimed too high, too soon. In one of the most upsetting moments, I learned that one senior investor had told a journalist: 'Who does this nigger think he is? There's no way we're going to let him do a transaction of $35 billion.'[5]

I remember a conversation with the boss of an external PR agency we used for communications around this time. He told me I should think about standing down. But I can say honestly that I never considered it. I knew I'd need to fight a skilled rearguard action, but having worked so hard to overcome so many barriers, I was determined not to see my career end like this. And although I hadn't sought to be, I knew I was a role model of sorts for many people. I felt like there was more riding on my career than my own success or failure.

As mentioned earlier, I did not seek to talk up my status as a role model. However, I'd received many kind and supportive messages in private from other black people since my unveiling as CEO. In moments after the AIG debacle, when my resolve and confidence were tested, I would think about the black cleaner I used to chat to on the executive floor of the Prudential building. One evening, as we both worked late, she confided that she had a picture of me in a frame at her house in her son's bedroom, and whenever her teen-age son did badly at school, or slacked off, she'd tell him to go take a look and aim as high as I had. Crashing and burning in such public fashion would send a terrible message to him and others.

I was bolstered by the fact that Prudential's figures for 2010 were the best ever in terms of profit and growth. I attended my first annual general meeting in early June to deliver a message that mixed contrition over the failed bid and optimism about the future. I set ambitious new growth targets for our businesses in Asia – the same targets that had been disbelieved by investors when we were promoting the AIA–Prudential merger. If we couldn't take over AIA, we needed to compete with them even harder.

There was one unresolved problem that was impossible to sugar-coat. Prudential faced costs of up to a billion dollars over the failed transaction, including a break-up fee that I had agreed with AIA, as well as lawyer and investment banking costs. I knew many shareholders were furious. I had done everything by the book: informing the chairman and board, gaining their approval, before pursuing the deal. Nevertheless, my comms advisors advised me to take a spare suit to the AGM in case anyone threw eggs at me.

I always have a plan in case of failure. When I had the deal approved by the board, I made an assessment of what a failed bid would cost, and had the board approve a budget for that: it was about GBP 1.5 billion. In the end, my CFO, Nic Nicandrou, who was heroic throughout the process, managed to negotiate the fees down to £450 million, which included the break-up fee. This was neither known nor understood by all those who wanted me fired. Chairman Harvey McGrath resisted intense pressure to throw me under the bus, at risk to his own reputation, before stepping down himself in 2012. I am indebted to him for his selflessness.

In October 2010, both of us were desperate to see how much AIA would raise when it floated on the Hong Kong stock exchange. After so many months of public criticism that we had offered too much, the market would give us the definitive verdict. The IPO valued the whole company at $30 billion and shares immediately jumped when they began trading. I had been almost spot-on. AIA was worth much more than this when combined with Prudential.

Was it a golden opportunity, as I explained again and again to sceptical shareholders, journalists and City analysts at the time? AIA is now worth $120 billion on a standalone basis.

The other repercussion from the aborted takeover was an investigation by the Financial Services Authority for Prudential failing to inform it of the takeover negotiations. The point at which traded companies must inform the regulator about takeover talks is a grey area, and many companies seek to delay as long as possible given how vulnerable such transactions are to leaks.

The FSA's investigation was time-consuming and immensely stressful, stretching over a period of three years. All of that time I faced the risk of a lifetime ban from the financial services industry and a fine of £400,000, which hung over my head like the sword of Damocles. It felt both unfair and intensely personal.

Firstly, the board had agreed with me that we were under no obligation to inform the regulator at the time because we had not submitted a binding offer. Given that it was a collective decision, the board wrote to the FSA and its then chief executive, Hector Sants, saying that any investigation should target the whole board rather than me personally because I had been fastidious in involving and keeping the board involved at all times. All decisions had been discussed and made collectively.

Sants replied that the FSA was at liberty to choose who it would indict and investigate – and they had decided to go after me alone. At one point, I was subjected to a ten-hour grilling from the Financial Crime Division. Sants seemed to enjoy reading me the riot act personally.

I was not alone in wondering why the FSA had singled me out. My supposed offence was one routinely committed by my peers for the exact same reasons: everyone knew the regulator couldn't be trusted to safeguard highly sensitive information. Many CEOs suspected the hedge funds had sources inside the FSA.

And there were far more egregious financial crimes worthy of prosecution. There had been no enforcement proceedings against the head of Royal Bank of Scotland, Fred Goodwin, who bankrupted the lender with the disastrous pre-crisis takeover of ABN Amro. Around the same time, bankers were fixing the London Interbank Offered Rate (LIBOR), a key benchmark interest rate. US sanctions against Iran were being breached. Everyone knew London was a giant laundromat for dirty money. My supposed 'crime' was committed over a deal that didn't happen.

In the end, three years later, the FSA announced its sanctions: Prudential was fined £30 million, the same amount handed out to Swiss bank UBS after one of their traders ran up a loss of £1.2 billion. And I became the only FTSE 100 chief executive to be given a public censure.

It made clear to me how, as a visible minority, I was vulnerable. I thought I was prepared and had always gone to great lengths to shield myself in ways that would be unimaginable for a white CEO in my position.

An American friend had once warned me that, as a black man in a senior position, people would try to catch me out on either money or sex. She quoted her former boss, the black politician Charlie Rangel who had once told her: 'They'll get you for a hamburger if they need to.' To guard against this, I asked for my expenses to be audited individually every year by KPMG. They went through everything I claimed from laundry bills to mini-bars.

When in the US, advised by my African American friends, I was always careful to avoid getting into an elevator alone with a white woman. If the elevator doors opened and there was a white woman alone, I would simply wait for the next one. Call it paranoia. Maybe. But I knew the word of a black man versus that of a white woman would not be worth much. It's depressing but statistically true. In a battle of her word against mine, if she accused me of assault, I knew I wouldn't be believed. For the same reason, I'm always scrupulously careful in avoiding any physical contact with female colleagues, ensuring I never inadvertently touch someone on the arm and reserving the French 'bise', the cheek-kissing greeting, for the closest of friends.

I was dogged by journalists chasing scandals throughout my time as Prudential CEO. I'm sure they felt there must be some-thing. I was a black man, right? If I wasn't embezzling cash, there had to be some scandal of one kind or another. This is how unconscious bias works in newsrooms. Editors who would be horrified to be called racist are prey to its effects.

At one point I had to fly out of London and hide in Barcelona because a British Sunday newspaper was preparing to publish a completely false front-page story about me having a relationship with my business manager, Amy. The irony was that I had gone to great lengths to protect myself while hiring a business manager, delegating the task to a company committee to remove any risk of being accused of bias.

I admired Amy, who was very smart, and I knew her husband, having invited them both to dinner to meet my wife. I signed an affidavit categorically denying any physical relationship, and she did the same. Given the lack of evidence presented by the newspaper – the whole story had been made up by a disgruntled former employee of Prudential – our lawyers managed to obtain a court injunction at midnight on the Saturday to block the article appearing the next day. Up until that point, I lay in my hotel room watching football, fearing my career was over.

When it wasn't sex scandals the press were after, it was evidence of potentially subversive behaviour. A few years later, when I was at Credit Suisse, *The Times* ran a story that I used to go clubbing with a colleague, Jean-Pierre Bouée, in Ibiza.[6] He and I to this day have never been clubbing together or even been to Ibiza, but this story got picked up and did the rounds among Credit Suisse investors. I am sure some to this day believe it to be true.

All that being said, I made no secret of my love of dancing! I will dance to anything – my parents adored dancing and my mother would often dance with me, waltzes, tango, rock 'n' roll. In many parts of Africa, including Ivory Coast, dancing has a completely different cultural significance than in Western European society. A man who can't dance, or at least won't make an effort to dance, is viewed with suspicion. Even if you're not any good, you're expected to enjoy it. Dancing means you're a master of your body, which is a projection of self-control, at least in many African cultures. At my first end-of-year staff ball, after I was appointed to lead the National Bureau for Technical Studies and Development in Abidjan – my first management position in Ivory Coast – employees were desperate to see if I could dance; I was expected to hit the dancefloor. And when I used to attend the World Economic Forum in Davos, I'd always be one of the last executives to leave the floor.

Despite the AIA failure, the FSA investigation and the at-times intrusive media reporting, I was happy in the UK. One of my friends who encouraged me to move over in 2003 had told me we were a good match for each other. She was right. I liked the humour, the sociability, London's music scene. I loved the sports culture too, as well as the general friendliness. I was struck by the kindness of the British as a people: when I had a knee operation and was visibly limping, people would stop and offer to carry my bags.

I was also stunned that I never got stopped, not once, by the police while driving in London. I do not mean to minimise the problem of racial profiling by security forces generally in the UK, which many campaigners remain concerned about. But the problem is a fraction of the one I encountered in France and in the US.

I also liked Britain's embrace of multiculturalism. Coming from France, I marvelled at the sight of public officials or police officers in headscarves, turbans or kippahs. British-born people of colour were at liberty to retain and celebrate some of their original culture without judgement or pressure. France's strict secularism and its insistence on cultural assimilation made all of this far more difficult.

In around 2010, I got a call from Clarence House. Prince Charles wanted me to join his Mosaic charity, which he had founded in 2007, and which provided mentoring for Muslim children from deprived backgrounds. It was the first time I'd met him, and I was so enamoured by his commitment – as surprising as it was admirable in my eyes – that I agreed right away to join the board. Many school visits followed. I was also invited to meet Queen Elizabeth II at Buckingham Palace.

My work for the G8, which had started with Tony Blair's Gleneagles summit in 2005, continued and expanded for the larger Group of Twenty (G20) countries, which included developing countries such as Brazil and India. My expertise was seen as useful in looking at ways to assist with African development, but also in harnessing the private sector globally to fight poverty. US president Barack Obama invited me to give a presentation on funding African infrastructure at the G8 that he was hosting at Camp David in May 2012.

Taking on all of these extra activities while running Prudential required mental bandwidth. That is one of the key requirements for CEOs – an ability to juggle several tasks at the same time and toggle between jobs almost instantaneously. It also helps if you don't need much sleep. I've only ever needed four or five hours a night.

As soon as the AIA merger debacle was behind me, I set about trying to grow Prudential in Asia. I faced a familiar foe there in the person of Mark Tucker, who had been named CEO of AIA after its IPO. Meeting my target of doubling profits in three years' time would require us to outshine him.

One of the big tweaks I pushed was selling our insurance products through banks. Prudential's model had always been to sell through its agents – known in the UK as 'The Man from the Pru'– which gave us higher profit margins and other advantages such as proximity to the client and greater control. But it also limited our scale. You can only expand as fast as you can train people, which takes time.

I wanted us to focus on Thailand, Indonesia, Vietnam, Singapore, the Philippines, and Hong Kong – what I called our 'sweet spots' in Asia. A lot of Western businesses looked at Asia and focused on mainland China and its one billion consumers. But these six countries comprised 750 million people and their business environments were considerably more friendly than China's. Demand was growing just as fast, far faster than we could provide for. I always told my teams that my 'dream pie' was a pie that expanded faster than I could eat it. If we could sell our products through banks in addition to agents, it would mean lower margins but still more value creation for our shareholders as were generating returns well above our cost of capital. Banks already had the clients. It was a simple next step to offer them insurance products. The cost to us of acquiring new customers was therefore very low.

One of the first major deals I completed was with United Overseas Bank in Singapore, which I negotiated personally with their owners. For a period in 2010, I was flying there every weekend for meetings. Other agreements followed, including one with Thai bank Thanachart. One of my last big deals as CEO was with Standard Chartered in 2014, when we paid more than a billion dollars to be their exclusive partner in all their branches across Asia for the next ten years.

We also bundled all of our products together, offering life insurance, health insurance and pension provision. In most Asian countries, the highest demand was for health insurance because public health provision is either unreliable or non-existent. People only drop their health insurance in extreme circumstances, meaning we could count on long-term loyalty.

I embraced building up the private health market as a public service – and I see no contradiction in this statement. My pitch to Asian governments would always be the same: they shouldn't seek to copy the post-war welfare systems of Europe, which I see as a huge long-term liability. They are increasingly financed by unsustainable borrowing, and amount to a huge subsidy for middle-class workers.

Why should a middle-class software engineer in Jakarta benefit from state-financed healthcare? The Indonesian government should focus on providing care for its poorest citizens. And once these people are provided for, there are so many other state spending priorities that should come before offering the software engineer free healthcare: education, infrastructure, law enforcement, environmental protection. Private health insurers and private providers are capable of delivering care more efficiently and at a lower cost to GDP than a catch-all, state-subsidised public system.

The other key development under my leadership of Prudential was the creation of an Asian wealth management arm, Eastspring, which was responsible for investing the premiums taken from clients and creating returns for them. So many people and policymakers wrongly believe banks provide the funds for private sector growth. Of course, they are a vital source of lending, helping lubricate the wheels of the economy. But it is insurance companies that create the deep pools of long-term capital that can be invested in companies and equity markets, providing the real engine for growth.

After two or three years at the helm at Prudential, I felt like the company was firing on all cylinders. The AIA takeover was a long-forgotten fever dream. In fact, looking back on it, it had helped bring the board together and laid the foundation for our success. Collectively we posted sixteen quarters of revenue growth of more than 16 per cent. We were like a German football team from the 1970s, sustained by our own winning momentum. During my time as CEO, the Prudential share price trebled.

My mother, who was full of the wisdom of our Baoulé tribe, used to say that it often didn't matter how anything started or what happened in the middle because no one remembers it. 'The only thing that matters in every endeavour in life is the end,' she'd say. It's the same with CEOs and their track records. I had had a terrible start, a good middle, and I knew that by 2015 I was on a high – the best time to bow out.

There had also been a change of chairman at Prudential in 2012. Paul Manduca, who was of Maltese origin and came from the fund management industry, had come in to replace Harvey McGrath. We worked quite closely as he was my chairman and the company had been through a traumatic time with the failure of the AIA transaction. We were chatting in his office when he said he imagined my family must be so proud of my achievements, which was a nice thing to say. Yes, I replied, of course. This reminds me of a conversation with a board director who will remain unnamed and who asked me, 'Did you ever think you'd have a white secretary?' I was dumbfounded.

In March 2014, when I received a vaguely worded invitation to meet one of the most powerful men in European banking via a headhunter, I sensed a new opportunity. The time had come to leave Prudential. I quoted my mother's proverb in my leaving speech at my last AGM. I left London with garlands. Sadly, I finished my next job in grime.

Chapter 6

Creditworthy

It was an uncertain courtship that took place over nine months and nineteen meetings into 2015. When relationships start out in complicated fashion, they often stay that way. This was no exception.

I knew the chairman of Credit Suisse, Urs Rohner, already. We both sat on the European Financial Service Roundtable (EFR), an industry lobby group that met a couple of times a year to discuss policy. We'd convene in a European capital for dinner, then have meetings the day after.

Urs stood out because he was always dressed in a three-piece black suit, with a shock of white hair and thick, dark-rimmed glasses. He was tall and retained the athletic build that had made him an elite-level hurdler and sprinter as a young man.

When I got a call from the headhunter in the spring of 2014, he suggested I might want to meet Urs formally. He didn't mention a vacancy, but I knew Credit Suisse was looking to replace their CEO, Brady Dougan, a former derivatives trader who had steered the bank relatively unscathed through the global financial crisis.

Urs kept the invitation vague, and I kept my intentions strictly to myself. We met first privately on the sidelines of an EFR meeting in Rome. Over the summer, several Credit Suisse board members flew to see me on holiday in Miami. Then Urs and I sat down again in London in mid-September.

I remember the time well because it was the day before the Scottish independence referendum. As we were having dinner together, my phone rang. It was the then UK prime minister, David Cameron. I excused myself to Urs and said I really needed to take the call. Cameron explained he was just back from his final campaign event in Edinburgh. He was desperate for any eleventh-hour public message against Scottish independence.

'You *have* to say something,' he told me.

The prime minister and I were on friendly terms, and I was a member of his business council. I found David smart and competent, on top of being good company.

'The day the British government needs somebody from Ivory Coast to opine on whether Scotland should remain part of the UK, you know you're in trouble,' I joked before agreeing to put a statement out via Prudential's press office.

Returning to my meeting, Urs seemed impressed. He pitched me the job strongly. We agreed to talk again and would see each other in Davos for the World Economic Forum in January 2015. Each time I raised reservations about the job, Urs returned with better and better offers.

I drove a hard bargain because I had serious doubts about the whole thing. I said I was only interested in taking the job if we were going to clean up the bank's practices. I told Urs how my reputation in the developing world was that of someone committed to fighting graft and corruption. I also told him that I thought helping money-launderers, tax dodgers and sanctions-busters was not a business model I wanted to get involved in: Credit Suisse had received a string of fines for behaviour that had inflicted major damage to its reputation and balance sheet.

Urs told me he agreed. He referred to the historic settlement the bank had just reached with US authorities – a $2.5 billion fine – for helping Americans evade taxes over the previous two decades. The deal would mean a US compliance officer and a large team sitting inside the bank to observe our practices. 'We've learned our lessons,' he promised.

But Urs was the former chief compliance officer. All of this, and much else, had happened on his watch. Would he and the rest of the board back me through the hard work of overhauling internal compliance processes and changing the culture inside one of Switzerland's most powerful institutions?

Despite these doubts, there was a real temptation to accept. Credit Suisse was a prestigious global brand and a major Wall Street player. Not many people are offered the chance to run a systemically important global bank, I told myself. There are only around thirty of them in the world. And no African had ever had an opportunity before. And there are 1.5 billion of us.

I knew I had one more CEO job in me after Prudential. Would I come to regret not taking Credit Suisse's hand? Was I going to get a better opportunity than this? I was also being offered attractive chairman positions – at drinks giant Diageo for instance. But at fifty-two, I didn't feel ready to become a chairman.

I've always been driven by a desire to stretch myself, to measure myself against the best. As a child I would constantly reach for new books in my father's library, looking to expand the limits of my knowledge. In government, I constantly strove for us to be more efficient, quicker, capable of acting at greater scale to transform lives. In business and management, I wanted to outshine my competitors, hit targets and please investors.

Whereas Prudential had been a growth assignment – expanding profits by growing the business in Asia – I knew Credit Suisse would be a restructuring job. That was a completely different challenge in nature and scale. And I would need to learn to operate in a different business culture. I've always admired José Mourinho as a football manager – not for the style of his teams, but because he has won championships in four different European leagues. That requires rare skill and emotional intelligence. Very few CEOs are capable of operating across boundaries in this way. Could I rise to the challenge, as a Morocco-educated Ivorian, a slightly reluctant Frenchman, and an adopted Brit? I felt the odds were not great, but it was difficult to pass up such a unique opportunity.

By this time, my boys had both grown up and left home. One was in his second year at Brown University, Rhode Island, after a gap year in Asia. The younger one was on a gap year in Asia, and on his way to university at Vassar in New York State. Annette and I had separated after twenty years of marriage. There was nothing in my personal life stopping me throwing myself into a new position in Zürich.

By February 2015, I still hadn't agreed to take the job after close to a year of back and forth. A sense of obligation descended on me that I allowed to cloud my judgement. I began to feel that Urs and the Credit Suisse board had invested so much in me that I owed them something in return. If I walked away, Urs would have a crisis on his hands.

There were nagging questions in my mind about the bank's culture and management style. I had a deep sense of foreboding, a feeling of contradictions left unresolved, which I ignored. I agreed to take the position.

The move was announced publicly in early March, on the day that I presented my final Prudential quarterly results – something I had now done twenty quarters in a row. Shares fell at Prudential and Credit Suisse's jumped, which was a reassuring vote of confidence in my abilities from the markets. I would remain Prudential CEO until June before starting my new job in Zürich on 1 July 2015.

After telling journalists there was 'no better time to leave' Prudential – profits were up again – I flew to Zürich to be officially unveiled at Credit Suisse's spectacular headquarters on the historic Paradeplatz. The reception was overwhelming on a personal level and extremely positive. I didn't realise what a big news story it would be internationally. There were television crews and journalists from all over the world. I had perhaps underestimated the role of investment banks in the public's mind. Their portrayal in popular culture through novels like Tom Wolfe's *The Bonfire of the Vanities* or films such as *The Wolf of Wall Street* mean they can inspire such strong feelings of admiration, jealousy and distaste. Insurance remains steady and rather dull by comparison.

The media coverage focused on my work at Prudential, how I was the bank's first francophone CEO and, of course, my skin colour. I was the first black CEO of a global European bank, as all the reports noted. The tabloid *Bilanz* even called me the 'Obama of Credit Suisse' and claimed my appointment demonstrated Switzerland's openness to the world.

I was needled at my first press conference by some questions about my supposed lack of experience in investment banking. The questions were to an extent understandable – I replied that I had plenty of experience of financial services through Prudential and McKinsey – but they also reflected some of the scepticism towards me in Zürich's tight-knit financial circles. I put it down to the traditional snobbishness of bankers towards insurance professionals. Prudential operated in the same industry as Credit Suisse. Yes, investment banking was a different part, providing different services to different clients. But we all operated with the same focus on interest rates, the yield curve and volatility. I was a specialist in risk management which, it seemed to me, Credit Suisse needed more than anything else.

Investment bankers still thought of themselves as masters of the universe, however. Only someone from their background could understand the formulas behind their securitised products and derivatives. But as I pointed out in my first press conference, referring to my years cramming at Polytechnique and the Ecole des Mines, 'I've studied maths and physics. Frankly the maths behind derivatives are a relative primitive form of that.'

As I was talking to the Swiss media, my phone rang: it was Aliko Dangote, Africa's wealthiest man. I called him back later. He had reached out to congratulate me. He said he was immensely proud that a fellow African had reached such an elevated position. If Aliko was ringing me personally and seemed delighted by the news, I felt I was in the right place. I also received a touching handwritten note from President Obama. 'Congratulations on the new job, Tidjane. I know you will excel,' he wrote.

To underline my commitment to the job, I started looking for a house to buy immediately. I intended to live in Zürich as a way of integrating myself socially, but also to signal that I was staying for the long haul. I found a villa in the southern commuter village of Herrliberg, with views out over Lake Zürich.

After thirteen years in the buzz of London, I was struck by the change in the pace of life in Switzerland. While I loved London, with its mash of messy architecture and mixed-up cultures, Zürich felt slightly isolated and sleepy at the end of its lake, flanked by mountains. If London was a global crossroads where people strove to stand out, Zürich was quite the opposite. I understood instinctively you were encouraged to fit in.

I thought I knew Switzerland before moving there. I had been to French-speaking Geneva many times both as a child with my mother and as an adult, a place where it was easy to feel at home as a foreigner among the UN agencies and other international organisations. But Zürich was different. My slightly rusty German language skills were rendered useless by the widespread use of Zürischnure, the local dialect. I found people to be courteous and welcoming, initially. One of my sons was the first to raise the alarm. He had come to live with me to do an internship at a Swiss law firm. He was troubled by the hostile looks from fellow passengers on the bus, and was regularly the only passenger to have his ticket checked, even though he was dressed in a business suit. Questioning by border police at the airport was often aggressive and rude.

'Watch out,' he told me as he left. 'This place is not nice.'

My first task was to conduct a deep strategic review of the bank. I intended to spend the first three months talking to people and working on a restructuring plan, which would be unveiled to staff and investors in October. I was also looking for managers to promote into new leadership positions.

I don't believe in coming into a company full of bravado and bluster, firing all the senior management and looking to create a board in my image. New strategies are often best when they are set by existing employees. Firstly, staff know the company best, which helps you avoid obvious and costly mistakes when you are at your most vulnerable as a new CEO. It also means your targets are more likely to be realistic and achievable. And thirdly, you have a better chance of employees throughout the organisation buying into the changes if they are seen as coming from within, rather than being imposed from the outside.

As a management consultant, I never encountered a problem in an organisation that could not be identified and resolved by people within it. The solution was always somewhere, but often stuck in a silo or business unit beyond the eyes and ears of senior management.

I did the same thing I have done since my first day at the bureau in Abidjan back in 1994: I toured Credit Suisse offices in person and held townhall meetings, in Zürich, London, Singapore, and New York. I also personally interviewed around sixty key people throughout the network, asking them all the same two simple questions:

'What do you think I should change?'

Most people were prepared for this and had elaborate answers at the ready. Meeting with a new CEO whose mandate was to shake up the company, they were quick to suggest reforms and changes, cuts, and consolidations.

And:

'What do you think I should not change?'

This was more difficult to answer, but the replies were equally illuminating. The conversation also felt more frank, less scripted. I wanted to identify the strengths: what worked, what merited being ringfenced and protected at a time when everything was under review. Working groups comprising senior management and promising middle managers were tasked with analysing and producing recommendations for the main components of my restructuring plan.

The first was for investment banking. For forty years, it had been the source of most of Credit Suisse's problems. I knew the board, investors and I all wanted to cut it down, but by how much? We also needed to reduce costs dramatically across the business; but where should we cut without inflicting self-harm? I wanted to switch our strategic focus to wealth management, but which markets should we target? How could we dramatically improve risk management and compliance? And what was the future for our Swiss business, the stable, boring but highly profitable domestic operation from which Credit Suisse had been derived?

While all of this was going on, I was delving further and further into the business. Before taking the job, I'd had dozens of conversations with Urs, as well as outsiders who knew Credit Suisse. I'd done the equivalent of walking around a second-hand car and checking its bodywork and basic functions before buying it. But it's only when you drive the car home that you can get under the bonnet and strip out the engine. What I discovered was not reassuring at all.

There were things I hadn't been told. There were things that were significantly worse than I'd been told. And there were things apparent to me about which people inside the bank were oblivious. It was going to be an even bigger job than I had ever imagined. I'd told Urs and the board that I thought the full restructuring would take ten years. This was starting to seem too optimistic.

One of the biggest uncertainties facing the bank was an outstanding case with the US Department of Justice over past mis-selling of residential mortgage-backed securities (MBSs) to investors during the period preceding the global financial crisis of 2008. Almost all major investment banks had been caught out peddling toxic assets based on subprime real-estate loans that they knew were riskier than advertised. US investigators possessed evidence from Credit Suisse employees referring to the loans as 'utter garbage' and 'complete crap'. The bank had been caught red-handed.

It became clear to me, after talks with Credit Suisse US lawyers, that we would need to set aside far more capital for this than I had been told and than the market generally believed. Urs had referred to a figure of around $5–8 billion. That would cover the federal settlement, but what they hadn't accounted for was all the other claims that come afterwards in the slipstream. We would have a long tail of subsidiary cases, involving states, municipalities and pension funds that were affected. The total figure was more likely to be $10–16 billion.

Urs had assured me in March that Credit Suisse was well capitalised. But as well as the US settlement, we also faced new regulatory pressure. After the financial crisis, banks were required by regulators to monitor and declare their risk-weighted assets (RWAs), a measure of their exposure to risk, which then determined how much capital they needed to set aside.

The problem was that many banks were gaming the system, seeking to find the riskiest assets possible with the lowest risk ratings, in order to maximise returns. So regulators, including the Swiss, brought in a second criterion – the leverage ratio – which measured the amount of equity versus the value of a bank's loan book.

On this latter measure, Credit Suisse was also caught with its pants down. The risk profile of our investment banking operations had increased by about 25 per cent in the previous two years. So not only was our risk-weighted assets ratio one of the worst in Europe; our leverage ratio was catastrophic. We needed to rectify it by raising capital urgently.

In October, I presented the restructuring plan. I made no apologies for the fact that it was bold and gutsy. The bank needed decisive action, not half-measures. We were going to cut investment banking, cut risk, and cut costs. And we needed to focus on growing the more stable, profitable and potential-rich business of wealth management, particularly in Asia.

Despite previous rounds of cost-cutting announced by management, I demonstrated that the bank's cost base had been reduced only marginally, from around 24 billion Swiss francs (CHF) in 2010 to 22 billion in 2014. At that level, our cost base was one of the highest in the industry. I set us a target of CHF 18.5–19 billion in 2018, a reduction of CHF 3.5 billion. I insisted we give an absolute figure, rather than the standard industry metric – the cost–income ratio – which can be more easily manipulated.

Bad cost-cutting is like dieting. As soon as you stop focusing on it, there's a risk that the weight comes back. This is what had happened in previous rounds. I wanted to focus on cutting fixed costs because they are real savings that don't reappear once your back is turned. Variable costs are easier to slash, but that does not have a lasting effect on the bottom line; only cutting fixed costs does, however it is, of course, much harder.

I spoke about the need to clear out offices. When you walk in and the building has been emptied, the computers are gone, the servers have been removed, and you hand back the keys to the lessor, that's real long-term savings. Our efforts also involved letting people go in some areas, but I wasn't interested in targeting headcount as a key metric. If you give a figure, it can create perverse incentives: positions are slashed, but then consultants are hired to replace them.

We had huge, stranded costs linked in many cases to financial products we had stopped selling. We were still sending out statements, maintaining client relations, the IT systems, often years or even decades later. I had a team dedicated to rooting out stranded costs and finding solutions: converting the products, paying customers off, or transferring their business to rivals. Only then could we decommission the servers, the customer support, and the IT systems.

And where we couldn't cut a fixed cost, we were wary. On a New York trading floor, if you reduce your traders from 200 to 190, you are still going to pay the same rent for the space, but you've just reduced your revenues. I couldn't afford to let revenues fall too quickly in the first year of the restructuring.

We also took care in identifying businesses that were non-strategic, but which were highly profitable. These included the securitised products division, which was run by a few highly talented people led by Brian Chin, an outstanding leader, someone I would very much rely on throughout my tenure. Their team consumed very little capital and generated $1.5 billion in annual profits. No one would pay us anywhere close to what it was worth to the bank. Selling it would simply have destroyed huge shareholder value. The division's sale after I left was a material mistake.

One area that was ringfenced from the cutting was risk and compliance. A scandal-plagued bank like Credit Suisse needed more internal controls, not less. Over the course of my tenure, we increased headcount in compliance by 40 per cent (contrary to some mistaken reporting on this issue). I also named a new head, Lara Warner, an investment banker who had been the highly successful CFO of the investment bank in New York. She would be my poacher-turned-gamekeeper.

Borrowing from my Prudential playbook, I also outlined how we would focus on expanding in emerging Asian markets. They were already the driver of the global economy and the region's new millionaires and billionaires, who were mostly entrepreneurs, needed two things from us: investment banking advice for their businesses, and private wealth management.

In the next five years, the global economy was expected to generate CHF 31 trillion in new wealth, with 60 per cent of that in emerging markets, above all in the Asia–Pacific region. In Asia, excluding Japan, more than half of this wealth would be first-generation entrepreneurs, according to Credit Suisse's own research. They should be our core target customer. As our new slogan stated, Credit Suisse would be a 'bank for entrepreneurs'.

As a mission statement, it encapsulated both my personal interests as CEO – serving entrepreneurs – and the interests of our shareholders. Part of the reason I took the job was because I was attracted by the wealth management industry and the chance to work with some of the modern-day titans of global capitalism, the great minds behind huge companies in China, Indonesia, Singapore or the Philippines who are largely unknown in the West. I would often fly to meet some of these ultra-high net-worth clients in person. Their trust was vital for our brand and helped encourage others to place their confidence in our asset managers. But their motivation in life was usually to grow their businesses, not to manage their wealth. So when they needed investment banking services – for an IPO, for loans secured against company assets, to arrange a private share sale – they would also turn to us and our investment banking division.

I was always fascinated by the Chinese billionaires in particular. As a teenager my father had made me read a book about China by Alain Peyrefitte, a French intellectual and a minister under President Charles de Gaulle. Published in 1973, it was titled: *When China Wakes Up, the World Will Tremble*, and it foresaw the transformation of the country, even as it struggled under the yoke of Maoism at the time.

I visited the People's Republic a decade later, in 1984, on an exchange trip financed by the French and Chinese governments that saw around thirty students from each country travel in both directions. China was just opening up under Deng Xiaoping, who was moving away from communist orthodoxy and incorporating free enterprise. Visiting was extremely difficult. We flew to Hong Kong then took a train to the mainland for a seven-week study trip around the country. We saw Beijing and Shanghai, of course, which are unrecognisable today from what they were then. We visited Xi'an, home of the buried terracotta army, as more and more figures were being excavated. We stopped in small regional cities which were usually off-limits to foreigners. Internal customs controls were so tight that you needed to fill in a form detailing all of your possessions – including the exact number of underpants, books, or medicines you were carrying – every time you crossed a provincial border.

Several things struck me. First and foremost was the poverty. At the time China's economy was worth around $250 billion, which per capita made it poorer than many African countries. The brutality of the Cultural Revolution under Mao was recent lived experience. The scars of the mass displacements, the forced agricultural work, the massacres, were still fresh. And yet you sensed communism had not changed the fundamental character of the country, or the deep identity of its people. You only needed to look at Taiwan, Singapore or Hong Kong to appreciate that the Chinese seemed to have an innate gift for business. When we visited universities and met other students, I was amazed at their ambition and reading of history. They were true believers in Deng's pro-market changes, and it is this generation that has driven the transformation of the country in the decades since. Many told me they were convinced that China was going to emerge from a period of weakness that they could trace back 300 years. Their poverty in 1983 was a historical accident.

The desperation of their fellow citizens – for food, for our oft-counted possessions, for foreign currency – was hard to miss. So was the sense of oppression, evident in how anyone who lingered near us in the street was whisked away by our official minders or plain-clothed police. We were entirely cut off from the world, with no access to foreign media. But I found the potential of the country mind-blowing, and I returned a changed person.

In my first meetings with prospective Chinese clients for Credit Suisse, I would often ask them what they were doing back then in 1984, when I visited as a student. Often they would tell me that their entire wealth then was a bicycle and the clothes they stood up in.

I saw wealth management and entrepreneurs like them as the future for Credit Suisse. Its vast trading operations were the past. To reduce our risk-exposure dramatically, I set up a 'bad bank' called the strategic resolution unit, whose task was to liquidate the bad loans, toxic assets and any other non-strategic businesses we owned, for the best price possible.

Many traders were reluctant to wind up loss-making positions, insistent that they would bounce back. I put one of the best of them in charge and offered him huge target-related bonuses for depleting the portfolio. In total, there were assets worth around $100 billion to dispose of, and the losses weighed on our results throughout my first years. A lot of European banks used the 'bad bank' structure to separate out unwanted legacy assets. We sold down ours at the lowest cost and at the fastest rate compared to other European banks, according to our own internal analysis.

The final spoonfuls of medicine were also unpalatable for different reasons. We needed new capital, so I proposed a share sale to raise another $6 billion, which would dilute the value of existing shares. Most radical bank restructurings are done with taxpayers' money once the institution has blown up. I was attempting to do one with shareholder funds. To everyone who fretted about the impact on the share price, I would reply that short-term losses to stockholders were preferable to bankruptcy, which would see the value of their investments wiped out. I had a problem, however: I had arrived in the job as someone who had trebled the share price of Prudential. Some people inside the bank promoted me as someone who could do the same at Credit Suisse, an impossible task in the short term for a woefully under-capitalised company with a history of scandals and excessively high costs.

Faced with such a daunting challenge, extreme measures were necessary. So, most controversially, I proposed an IPO of the domestic Swiss bank to sell a 20–30 per cent stake to investors. This was previously unthinkable. Inside and outside the bank, many people thought we were pawning the family jewels. But I needed to reassure investors that we had quick ways of raising more cash if necessary. Any doubts about our capital position as a bank could be fatal (as the ultimate demise of Credit Suisse demonstrates).

Given the scale of the shake-up and the tacit admission of our capital shortages, I was seriously concerned about the share price reaction after the restructuring plan was unveiled. A huge fall was to be expected, if nothing else because of our plan to issue 260 million new shares. It fell 6 per cent on the day. It was bad, but better than we expected.

Our CFO David Mathers oversaw the work of the 'bad' bank, meaning I could focus on the 'good' one which, in the first few months, meant focusing on the downsizing of the investment banking activities and upscaling wealth management. I received two nasty surprises before I could present the final year results in February 2016.

The first stemmed from the actions of a group of traders on our distressed debt desk in New York. The desk comprised a handful of very specialised brokers who bought and sold the debt of companies that were near or going through bankruptcy proceedings. It's extremely high-risk, high-return trading. Four or five of them had racked up losses that eventually totalled $1.5 billion by taking bad positions just before interest rates started to rise. Having blown through internal limits, their managers and risk controllers had authorised them to keep going deeper into the red in the belief that the positions would eventually turn around. As so often in trading scandals – and losses in casinos – the attitude was to keep playing and hope no one noticed.

I ordered an internal investigation. The incident raised questions about our internal processes, but also broader issues about what sort of institution we wanted to be in the future. I was personally furious. I'd just worked round-the-clock to try to convince investors to buy $6 billion in fresh equity, persuading them to believe in my strategy, and a few people on a trading desk in New York had lost a quarter of that amount. They had no idea how hard it was raising money.

As a consequence, I closed the distressed debt trading desk. My view was simply that a systemically important bank like Credit Suisse had no business doing such high-risk trading. The logical operators in such a market are hedge funds, which are gambling with their own money. They are not using the deposits of 'mom-and-pop savers' and small businesses back in Switzerland and are ultimately not backed by the Swiss taxpayer. Trading distressed debt was outside of my risk appetite, so my view was that it was better to close it immediately and take the hit, rather than see our exposure worsen. My mantra is that if you don't like a risk, don't own it. Closing the operation also sent a clear message to others: if you break my risk management rules, there will be consequences.

I also wanted to underline one of my core management beliefs. There is a tendency for many CEOs and managers to want to control as much as possible. It's driven by a desire for self-preservation and is understandable given that the buck always stops with them. But it often results in overreach and staff who feel disempowered. I have always favoured the opposite and pushed for decisions to be sent to their lowest level possible. But there is a crucial condition: if you empower people and trust them to make decisions, they need to know the importance of escalating information to the executive level. With autonomy comes responsibility.

I would always say to my teams that good news always travels fast inside companies. Success has many fathers, as the old saying goes. Everyone is keen to tout their achievements. But I wanted bad news to travel even faster than good news. I would tell managers that I knew that there would be moments when they'd wonder if they should share something with me. In those situations, there are two risks people need to worry about: if you tell the CEO something that he doesn't need to know, the damage is limited. But if you don't tell the CEO something they needed to know, then the damage is potentially infinite. The rational approach is to always err on the side of caution and to 'overshare'.

The distressed debt debacle at the end of 2015 at Credit Suisse was a case study in what can go wrong with decentralised decision-making. When the traders began racking up losses, the risk oversight committee should have stepped in to instruct them to close their positions. But instead it extended their trading limits, despite the market moving against them. This decision was never escalated to more senior management. The circle of people who knew that the bank was taking on huge new liabilities was incredibly small until it was too late. The head of markets only found out once the losses had accumulated, the CFO even later, and finally me.

The episode also underscored how the incentives for Wall Street traders are so often not aligned with the interests of their organisation and its shareholders. It's a cliché, but true, that traders are primarily motivated by personal enrichment and short-term gain. When they make money, they hit their targets and unlock their bonuses. The problem is when they lose it. The risks are asymmetric. When they take bad positions, the bank picks up the tab. More often than not, it even ends up paying out their bonuses anyway, out of fear that the so-called talent will jump ship to a competitor. It's a rigged casino. The rewards and costs are completely unbalanced and disproportionate. And it encourages a culture of risk-taking.

We had another incident in late 2018. After the distressed debt debacle, it became one of my sacrosanct rules that we were not to take major risks on financial markets at the end of the year. Disasters often occur in November and December for the simple reason that investment managers are trying to hit their annual targets. They start feeling pressure and take inconsiderate risks. For me as CEO, I didn't want a major change in our trading position that put our performance over the previous ten or eleven months in jeopardy.

During our annual investor day, at the end of 2018, I got a call from New York saying we faced a $60 million loss on a block trade in shares in Canada Goose, the Canadian luxury outerwear maker. Canadian authorities, responding to a US warrant, had arrested Huawei executive Meng Wanzhou in early December. China had threatened retaliation and shares in Canada Goose, which was highly exposed to the Chinese market, had tanked. The upside on that trade to the company was probably $500,000, which we'd probably end up spending on bonuses anyway. In the end, shareholders took the hit – again.

I was often accused of having a bias against Credit Suisse's investment banking operations. But tracing back the demise of Credit Suisse, it is clear that so many of its troubles, including its final sad denouement, stemmed from its desire to be a player on Wall Street. That desire had led to disastrous acquisitions, poor management, and a totally defective risk culture.

One of those disastrous acquisitions came back to haunt me in my first three months in the job. In September 2000, Credit Suisse had purchased the New York brokerage Donaldson, Lufkin & Jenrette, for $11.5 billion – an astronomical figure, several times the value of the company's assets, made at the height of the dot-com boom. We were still carrying goodwill on the balance sheet from that transaction.

Given the downsizing of our investment bank division, I came under pressure from the head of the audit committee, John Tiner, who had been there for more than ten years, to suddenly write down the value of the goodwill by $4 billion in the final quarter. This is something the bank had lived with for a long time. For reasons that were unclear to me, it suddenly became urgent to tackle the issue. It would ruin my first results. I couldn't understand why they were making me, a new CEO, carry the can for a doomed decision made fifteen years earlier. That wasn't customary corporate behaviour. Why hadn't they written it off before, at the end of my predecessor's term, for example?

I argued. We went back and forth with the chair of our audit committee in vain. In the end, I had to announce a fourth-quarter loss of more than CHF 6.4 billion, almost all of it caused by the distressed debt sale and the writedown.

My relationship with the bank's chairman began to feel strained only a few months into my time there. I felt that Urs had failed to be frank with me about the scale of the problems. When I raised the writedown or the under-capitalisation issue, he protested that they had been too sensitive to discuss until I joined the company. I was beginning to wonder whether I'd been brought in as a fall guy – someone to do the clean-up tasks; a sanitation worker in the CEO's office who would be disposed of once he had swabbed the floors.

I focused on my restructuring plan, step by step, with every component subject to regular monitoring. Some people looked at the cost-cutting and growth targets and concluded they were unreasonable – mountains they couldn't climb. I set around fourteen objectives internally that were within our grasp. I've always tried to run companies based on a relatively small number of metrics. I've also ensured my executive team is small too, numbering five or six. We'd have larger board meetings regularly, but I'd notice the difference in the quality of the debate. Smaller groups almost always lead to freer and more constructive discussions.

Once I set objectives, I am single-mindedly focused on achieving them. I created a committee for monitoring the restructuring process. Any time an issue came up that they couldn't resolve immediately, they were empowered to escalate it to the executive board. We had a reporting system with traffic lights, which indicated whether we had hit our objectives or not. We tracked targets every day, every week and every month for three years. When we needed to make adjustments or correct course, we did. That's how you make unreasonable progress. All the time, I had teams who enjoyed the freedom, autonomy and rewards offered by our decentralised management approach.

I was also steadily accumulating enemies. There was pushback from within the investment banking unit, which was foreseeable. I was cutting jobs and, more importantly, bonuses, and downgrading the status of investment bankers within the bank. There had always been tensions between New York and headquarters and I was determined to show who was in charge.

At the beginning of 2016 I made myself very unpopular by slashing the 2015 bonuses given the catastrophic annual results. I was the first CEO to dare to do this. My view was that the results were bad and so the bonuses weren't justified. Yet these supposed arch-capitalists protested. Those who wanted to be paid with money the bank did not have showed a level of selfishness and cynicism I had not encountered in my career until that point. Many of them badmouthed me on the pages of the *Wall Street Journal*. Some journalists told me afterwards that during that time all they had to do was go stand on the kerb in front of our 11

Madison Avenue headquarters and traders would pour out cursing me.

I love markets because they have consequences. You pay too much, you lose money. You make a bad investment, you take a hit. You run your business badly, you go to the wall. Every decision, good and bad, sends signals to others. Capital is gradually allocated productively. If you remove the consequences of a bad call, you remove any incentive to improve. You trade badly, you don't get your bonus. That's how you stop being a casino with one-way bets. 'I'm aware that I'm not very popular right now,' I told a conference in Zürich in March. 'But it's not my job to be popular.'

In Switzerland, my efforts to clean up our private banking operations ran into internal and external resistance. The model of Swiss banking used to rely on the principle of no-questions-asked service and a guarantee of anonymity. After the global financial crisis, which led to new transparency demands and strong regulation, that model faced evident problems. There was growing international pressure, particularly to crack down on tax dodgers, which had cost Credit Suisse $2.5 billion in the United States the year before I joined. We had an American compliance officer with a very large team sit inside the bank as part of our settlement. Several months into my tenure, we settled with Italian authorities over historic tax claims.

We had also been fined for sanctions-busting in Sudan and Libya. We took another hit from the actions of corrupt bankers in Mozambique. Between 2004–08, in an infamous criminal case, the bank had accepted millions from a former Bulgarian wrestler turned cocaine dealer. Each time our reputation took a further hit.

Furthermore, the world, and social attitudes, had changed. Governments were desperate for tax revenues after the global financial crisis; and voters felt increasingly disgusted about rich people dodging taxes. There was also a growing trend of disgruntled employees handing over confidential data to journalists and foreign tax authorities, rendering the anonymity supposedly guaranteed by Swiss banking law a chimera.

I wasn't foolish enough to think I was going to clean up Swiss banking culture overnight, like Hercules diverting rivers into the Augean stables. But my argument internally was that taking on clients who were high risk and seeking to use the bank to hide illicit wealth was simply bad business. The downside was potentially huge, and the upside was limited. Our future lay in above-board wealth management for legitimate entrepreneurs who had earned their savings.

I wanted data to back up this intuition, so I worked with Palantir, the US software group, to help us identify so-called 'politically exposed' clients. We were initially looking for the archetypical kleptocrat – a developing world civil servant or minister with wealth far exceeding their known sources of income. We also looked for obvious tax evaders.

What we found was that most of them were holding relatively small sums which carried huge reputational risk. We closed thousands of accounts in total, including 15,000 belonging to French people, and removed $40 billion of dirty assets during my time. The work with Palantir was also useful in helping us comply with sanctions. I discovered that whenever new measures were announced by European powers or the US – against Iranians, Syrians, or Russians, for example – I'd ask whether we were exposed, and it would take three months to get an answer from my colleagues. How can you manage your reputational and financial risk as a bank if you don't know who your clients are and how much money they hold with you?

There was a limit to how much we could do in a short time: I always made the same analogy to foreign regulators when they asked about my intentions. I told them I thought of myself as running a farm. Some of their cows had run away because of a breach in my fence. I would do my best to catch the cows.

However, the most urgent task was fixing the fence so the problems would not get worse. Catching the escaped cows had to come second to that. Given the limits to the firm's resources in the middle of a restructuring, I felt it was wrong of regulators to focus on making us pay for the mistakes made by previous managements, stopping us from being able to invest in avoiding future accidents.

But, as I discovered, it is one thing to have rules, procedures and staff, it's another to change the culture of an organisation. As soon as I joined, I would see how senior managers in the wealth management business would ask for 'overrides' – permission to ignore due diligence requirements – to bring new clients on board or protect existing ones. I remember at one of our weekly executive board meetings we were asked to arbitrate in a case involving an Israeli-American businessman who we had reason to believe was evading US taxes. There was a tussle between the head of our Israel desk, who wanted to shield the client, and the general counsel, who wanted to uphold the law.

I suspended the head of the Israel desk and asked that we report the individual immediately. I later discovered that US authorities were aware of the case and had been waiting to see whether Credit Suisse had learned the lesson of its tax evasion settlement. They were reassured by my actions, helping raise trust after so many scandals in the past.

As CEO, I never invoked powers to override compliance procedures to onboard a client and I had many arguments with Urs about this issue. I didn't even want the power. My view was that the rules should be the same for everyone, however big the potential financial reward. Managing dirty money was no longer the bank's business.

We were apparently losing clients to competitors such as the Julius Baer Group. One of my predecessors, Oswald Grübel, a doyen of Zürich banking, said that compliance was an 'Anglo-

Saxon' concept that was foreign to the Swiss. Like others, he suspected it was part of a plot by jealous American and British peers to bring down the Swiss banking industry.

The more I pushed, the more I noticed unpleasant Swiss media reports about me, focusing on my supposedly ostentatious lifestyle, fed by people upset about job cuts or strategy. I drove a Porsche Cayenne, said one piece. I had been spotted flying first-class, said another. I often used suites in hotels during foreign travel. I was getting divorced …

As for the substance, a Porsche Cayenne is hardly a flashy vehicle in Switzerland. My assistant drove one, as did many mid-level executives in the bank, who also flew first-class for long-haul travel. Many of those hostile stories were spread by people riding around in Ferraris or Porsches. Maybe it was simply that a Porsche Cayenne was 'too much' for a black man. And I have used hotel suites to hold meetings early or late in the day since my time as a management consultant in the early 1990s.

The stories were insignificant, silly even, when looked at individually. But what they revealed as a whole was a double standard: Which other CEO in Switzerland faced such intrusive press coverage? I also received racist messages and death threats in my mailbox at home, saying things like: 'Go back to Africa, Nigger.' I told Urs about it. He urged me to ignore it. 'I get hate mail too,' he said, as if being insulted was the same as being racially abused. I saw the same insensitivity at his sixtieth birthday party in late 2019, which had a 1970s theme. A black performer came on stage dressed as an office cleaner, dancing as he pretended to sweep the floor. Some of Urs's friends performed songs in front of us in 'Afro' wigs.

The year 2016 was the worst. We had frontloaded all the most painful restructuring work, hoping to complete the hardest parts in the first year. If you try to restructure in equal parts every year, you'll fail. We did 50 per cent of the cost cuts and other changes in year one, including liquidating assets in the 'bad bank'.

At the start of the year, I reached a deal with President Obama's attorney general, Loretta Lynch, to finally settle the US Department of Justice case dating back to the mis-selling of mortgage-backed securities between 2006–08. It was a turning point for me as Credit Suisse CEO, because for the first time I was able to put a figure on a liability the bank had been carrying for years.

It was an uncommon feeling to go to meet Lynch in Washington and plead for clemency. The size of the settlement boiled down to whether she believed me when I said Credit Suisse had changed and that the mis-selling reflected errors that could not be repeated. Her department had talked about a figure of $7 billion.

I brought plenty of evidence of how we were investing in risk and compliance. I stressed how our capital position remained precarious and I simply wasn't sure whether we could pay a huge fine that would force me to raise more money from shareholders who might reject another rights issue. I had further meetings with assistant attorney general, Bill Baer, who was in charge of the MBS settlements. He had a reputation as a rottweiler character who would yell at CEOs and humiliate them. I suspect my not being an investment banker helped, as well as our shared past experiences at the World Bank. In any case, he was polite and seemed to believe me when I said I was changing Credit Suisse's course.

The final settlement figure of $5.8 billion, with only $2.48 billion immediately payable, was at the lower end of expectations. Our general counsel called the negotiation a 'Houdini act'. It was the second-smallest settlement, after JP Morgan Chase's, of all the investment banks caught up in the mis-selling scandal.

The most immediate consequence was that I could call off the IPO I had announced for the Swiss national bank in my restructuring plan in October 2015. It knew it was unpopular, and had always intended it to be my final card – played only if we were desperate for additional capital and had no other choices. We announced its cancellation shortly afterwards.

The year also threw up two political earthquakes to deal with: Donald Trump's election as US president and Brexit in the UK. Brexit didn't come as a surprise. One of the things I noted very early in my time in Britain was how the country felt disconnected from Europe – evident in how English people would talk about travelling 'to Europe' or 'to the continent' whenever they took the Eurostar. On the US elections, I'd spoken to Rupert Murdoch beforehand, who was convinced Trump would win. After watching and analysing the campaign, I came to the same conclusion.

None of my early years at Credit Suisse had been easy. At no point did I feel I could relax, given the scale of the challenges. But there were signs, by my third year in charge, that the strategy was on track and things were starting to click. The US government liability was settled. The bad bank was being wound up. Our investment banking operations were being downsized and de-risked at pace. The Swiss bank was booming. In my first four years, we saw $200 billion in new funds flow into our wealth management business. Such was the speed of the turnaround that the *Euromoney* magazine named me Banker of the Year in 2018. It was in recognition of my efforts which had 'reinvented Credit Suisse with wealth management at its core'.[1] It was a repudiation of the critics who had suggested I wouldn't be able to understand banking.

To my eternal chagrin, I was never able to complete the turnaround work. After the difficult cutbacks and restructuring, I could clearly see us taking an upward trajectory that had been a hallmark of my time at Prudential. In 2020, I presented the best full-year results for the bank in ten years, with nearly USD 4.0 billion in pre-tax profits. During my time in charge, we had also raised around $11 billion (CHF 10 billion) in fresh capital from shareholders and reduced our annual cost base by around 20 per cent.

I told Urs when I first took the job that I thought I would need ten years. I was in my fifth, only halfway, when I was forced to resign.

The events that led up to my departure have been described in detail elsewhere. As I stressed in my introduction, this book was never intended to be an opportunity to settle scores or conduct an anatomy of my tenure. For legal reasons, but above all out of a sense of personal propriety, I will not elaborate in detail on my final months, but will lay out the established facts and give my thoughts on the wider significance of events.

I left Credit Suisse in early February 2020 under immense media and internal pressure over a so-called scandal dubbed 'Spygate' in the Swiss and international media. It stemmed from a decision by the bank's security services – a department that existed prior to my tenure and had remained unchanged – to put a disgruntled former employee under surveillance.

That employee, Iqbal Khan, was a man I had promoted to head of our international wealth management (IWM) division after I joined in 2015. He had done a very good job as part of my team in charge of defining a new strategy for the bank. Creating IWM was one of the signature moves of my tenure, and it proved very successful in driving profitable growth. It was basically our Swiss offshore business, which I had separated from the onshore Swiss bank.

My relationship with Iqbal had soured over the years for various reasons, some personal. I had given Iqbal a huge career boost and he was someone I had great hopes for. A series of incidents, some of them simply bizarre, impacted our relationship. One of them involved derogatory comments made by one of Iqbal's key lieutenants about me at an IWM event. This was escalated by colleagues, who were shocked that this individual would speak in such a way about his CEO, and was investigated by HR and compliance, who concluded that this was a serious incident.

I called Iqbal into my office to brief him and ask what he was going to do about it. He told me he didn't plan to do anything, which I grudgingly accepted. I was then surprised to see that someone had given an account of that conversation in the Swiss media saying that I had asked Iqbal to 'dig up some dirt' on the employee. That is simply a lie. I never said such a thing and there are enough witnesses to confirm this. This was typical of the media campaign against me that took place almost daily for more than a year during this time.

A few months before he resigned, there were reports that Iqbal had gone to Julius Baer, one of our key competitors, and shopped around a list of clients and staff he could bring with him. Such a story was highly damaging for Credit Suisse. I asked Urs, who was close to Iqbal, to issue a story denying the allegations. He flatly refused to do so. I was shocked that nothing was done.

When Iqbal announced that he was leaving Credit Suisse to join our main competitor UBS, the bank's security services, overseen by chief operating officer Pierre-Olivier Bouée, identified a risk of him poaching clients and violating the terms of a three-month non-competition agreement. They ordered discreet surveillance.

This surveillance was entirely legal under Swiss law. Corporations use security services for a host of legitimate reasons, from running background checks on potential new hires to investigating leaks of sensitive information. Many former law enforcement officers are employed in this industry. One of their missions is to help protect commercially valuable information.

Iqbal was never in any personal danger. In the flood of often inaccurate information afterwards, some reports falsely claimed he was physically threatened. An internal bank inquiry concluded I had not been personally involved in the decision to monitor Iqbal.

So where was I culpable? I certainly underestimated the intensity of the media coverage. Even though I knew how, as a black

CEO, I faced greater scrutiny and was more vulnerable than my white peers, I still believed that as I delivered good financial results the pressure would at some point fade. It never did.

I raise the issue of race here reluctantly again. Journalists have asked me for years to give an interview about it. I have always said no. My rationale is that there are two kinds of people in the audience for such an interview: those who are racist and prejudiced, and those who are not. The ones who are not, do not need to be lectured. The ones who are prejudiced would just accuse you of playing 'the race card': that argument is one of the most potent ones concocted to use against minorities who dare to talk about racism.

In a *Financial Times* article published around the time of my departure, one of my fellow board members – unnamed, of course – said that 'Tidjane saw race everywhere'.[2] The choice of this line, so popular with racists, was highly unfortunate. It is exactly because of this type of attitude that I'd never called out the racism publicly.

In retrospect, perhaps I failed to react sufficiently quickly and strongly to events. My biggest mistake was misreading the Zürich microcosm and the Swiss more broadly, failing to understand that they were determined to see me out of that job, at any cost. If it had not been the surveillance, it would probably have been something else.

The bank's supposed offence was not an offence in a legal sense, I reasoned. It seemed to me to be far less serious than the long-standing use of Credit Suisse accounts by senior former Third Reich officials hiding in Argentina – the existence of which was discovered at about the same time – or the mass concealment of Jewish assets looted by Nazis. These did not raise an eyebrow in the German-speaking Swiss media. It was certainly less significant than instances of actual law-breaking, such as sanctions-busting and money-laundering for war criminals or drug dealers. And what about the mass facilitation of tax dodging?

All of these were part of Credit Suisse's recent and not-so-distant past. None of them were deemed to be as culturally unacceptable and resignation-worthy for my predecessors or other people still on the board.

I had never worried too much about my image or PR throughout my career, choosing instead to focus on delivering good results. My mantra was that: 'If you don't deliver, there is no amount of good PR that will rescue you. And if you deliver, there is no amount of bad PR that can kill you.' Well, it turned out I was wrong about that. I didn't have to step down for bad performance.

No previous CEO in charge of a Swiss bank had faced anything like the same opprobrium. What's more, my so-called scandal was also the only one that hadn't cost the company's shareholders any money. I'm sure this is why our largest investor, David Herro, was adamant that I should stay in my job.

It is up to others to judge the extent to which forcing me out halfway through my restructuring was to blame for the bank's failure. I'm often asked why, over the long term, Credit Suisse had been so plagued by scandals, which brought about its ultimate demise. In the final analysis, it's to do with culture, both inside and outside the bank. There are vices inherent in some Swiss bankers: their sense of impunity, of privilege, their belief that ultimately no one will ever find out; and even if they do, the consequences will be minimal. It's easy to see how that breeds secrecy and contempt for rules. Wall Street has its own vices: the bombast, the avarice, the reckless risk-taking. For four decades, Credit Suisse straddled these two worlds: the quiet, conservative, look-the-other-way discretion of Zürich banking, and the brash, masters-of-the-universe mentality of New York trading. It could never reconcile them. And both legs were deeply infected with a rot that only a sustained, long-term effort could root out.

I used to give a speech internally during my time as Credit Suisse CEO which summed up how I felt. It became known as the 'toilet speech' and would often follow another frustrating screw-up: a bad trade, a misguided decision to onboard a questionable client, or a failure to alert managers or regulators about risk-taking.

I would tell traders and wealth managers that I was like one of the workers who cleaned their offices, the guy with the mop and fresh towels. I had been brought in with a specific task: to swab the toilets because people had been literally defecating all over the floor. This would prompt awkward smiles and nervous laughter.

I'd tell them that over my years, I'd cleaned up. I'd built the best toilets, Japanese-style ones, with heated seats, jets, sprays, and perfume. They're the most comfortable lavatories available. Everyone can use them.

'But some people keep shitting on the floor. Perhaps they think it's fun. Perhaps they can't kick their old habits. But please, please, please, from now on use the toilets,' I'd plead.

What I meant was that everyone needed to respect the new rules and spirit of the bank. Stop doing dodgy business like a secretive Swiss banker who imagines no one will find out. Or taking risks like a Wall Street trader who thinks there will be no consequences for reckless risk-taking.

As every plumber knows, one of the drawbacks of the profession is that sometimes you get sprayed. When the Credit Suisse toilets backwashed, I found myself alone, standing in other people's sewage. My earliest intuition – that I had been brought in to be a fall guy – only hardened.

The rationale I was given by the board was that I had done an excellent job but 'the press campaign against me would never stop', so I had to go. I objected that the bank was run for its shareholders, not the German-speaking Swiss press. Furthermore, a lot of that famous 'media campaign' was being fed by some Credit Suisse board members.

For Credit Suisse's shareholders, the decision to force me out before I could complete the turnaround would prove catastrophic.

I left without even being asked to organise an orderly transition with my successor. I was out of the bank within five days and flabbergasted that the regulator would not object to this, whatever my apparent faults. My successor would have benefited from time learning about some of the things to particularly watch out for. What the bank needed most, it was denied: continuity and steady strategic direction.

I want to end this section with a comment of a personal nature, the inclusion of which I have thought long and hard about. In November 2018, my eldest son was diagnosed with Stage 3 cancer, non-Hodgkin Lymphoma. I immediately informed Credit Suisse's chairman and the board. They agreed that dealing with this should be my priority.

I was asked to continue in my job though. One of the things I found particularly upsetting about my final year in charge was that some of the worst behaviour and leaking to the media was done by people with the knowledge that my son was dying. It ended with the news of his death in May 2020 being given to the Swiss tabloid *Blick*. I am sure I am not the first CEO in that country to lose a child to cancer. But I don't know of another case in which it was announced in the tabloids, with pictures of the deceased.

In 2023, there were further attempts to demonise me, with a campaign to pin blame on me for Credit Suisse's ultimate failure. If I had committed such grave mistakes, how come they were not spotted in the three years after I left, by either the regulators or the board or management? I will leave the final word on this to Duncan Mavin, a British journalist who recently published an illuminating book called *Meltdown*: 'It's impossible,' Mavin wrote, 'to think that the criticism that he faced in light of the collapse of the bank doesn't also reflect the xenophobia, racism and snobbery that Thiam encountered while in charge.'[3]

Chapter 7

Africa's Century

After leaving Credit Suisse, I turned down a number of offers to become CEO or chairman of major European companies, including UniCredit, the Italian bank. I had no desire to put my feet up, however. The world of work animated me just as much as it always had. But I wanted to work differently.

I accepted a handful of board positions as an independent director, as well as a role working on behalf of the African Union, as an envoy to coordinate Africa's response to Covid-19. I also began working with start-ups, as well as promoting entrepreneurship and innovation in Africa. My main personal business focus became setting up a so-called SPAC investment fund for acquisitions in the United States, which we listed on the New York Stock Exchange.

In 2022, I made a trip that would change me: I returned to Ivory Coast for the first time in more than twenty years. It came at a time of growing instability in West Africa and the neighbouring Sahel region. Countries were falling prey to a string of coups. In recent years, military men have overthrown elected governments in Guinea, Mali, Burkina Faso, Niger, and Gabon.

It worried me to read about how these changes had often been welcomed by many people. Surveys showed that faith in democracy as a system of governance was falling in Africa, as it was in much of the West. According to Afrobarometer, a pan-African polling group, the share of Africans who prefer democracy to any other form of government fell from 75 per cent in 2012 to 66 per cent in 2024.[1] That is still solid backing, but the fall reflects disillusionment with the manner in which many countries have been administered. As victims of wars, terrorist groups and poverty, many Africans are entitled to ask whether the system is working for them.

Too often African leaders pay lip service to the fundaments of democracy – the elections, the need for opposition parties, a free media – but do not respect the spirit or practice of it. Electoral lists are purged, padded, or restricted. Opposition parties are permitted to exist merely as fall guys in a national masquerade. The media is manipulated or cowed. Afrobarometer survey results show that only 37 per cent of Africans were satisfied with the way democracy works in their country in 2024.[2]

From my viewpoint, straddling both France and Britain, and Africa and Europe, I am also struck by the growing differences between francophone and anglophone countries in Africa. I'm convinced it reflects something deeper about how we experienced colonialism.

In former British East Africa, power changes hands in a mostly orderly manner in countries such as Kenya and Tanzania. Ex-French colonies in West Africa are, by contrast, a governance graveyard. Since the turn of the century – according to data from Jonathan Powell and Clayton Thyne, political scientists at the University of Kentucky, who maintain a database – eighteen out of twenty-four coups in Africa have taken place in francophone countries. Since 2020, it is eight out of nine.[3]

The reasons for this are multiple and complex. Coups often have local dynamics, with many formerly French countries in the Sahel badly destabilised by an upsurge in Islamist terrorism over the last decade. But it is impossible not to conclude that the political and economic cultures left behind by the former colonial powers also appear to play a part in the diverging fates of anglophone and francophone Africa.

Britain's colonialism was different to France's in several crucial ways. It was often indirect, using vassalised local elites to be the public face of power when all the strategic decision-making was made back in Whitehall and Westminster in London. Though cynical and cunning, it offered a degree of local autonomy which empowered a small local elite. It was also more capitalist and business-oriented in nature, with colonisation often carried out by private companies and traders under the protection of British guns.

That helped create a class of black business people, the legacy of which you can see in places such as Nigeria or Kenya today. The real profits were reserved for white people, of course, but business provided a route to success for a small number of enterprising Africans. That route did not exist in places like Ivory Coast.

The French empire-builders were usually military men. And the French system was state-directed occupation and extraction, dressed up with self-serving baloney about spreading civilisation and Catholicism to the grateful natives. Where French-occupied African territories were not considered simple extensions of mainland France – in the case of Algeria, for example – they were directly administered by Paris. The route to power and wealth in colonial French-speaking Africa ran through the state bureaucracy.

When the first major wave of decolonisation occurred in the 1950s and 1960s, Britain found it easier to hand over power and leave, both on a practical and philosophical level. France clung on, fighting a traumatic and brutal war to retain Algeria and manoeuvring to maintain its political, economic and military hegemony in its former territories ever since.

Until very recently, France still had a string of military bases across West Africa and the Sahel region, which have been used to support friendly regimes. It had around a thousand troops in Ivory Coast. Its companies remained major players in a host of strategic sectors, where for decades they expected to be given preferential treatment, as I saw with my own eyes when in government.

In economic affairs, fourteen African countries still use the CFA, a currency backed by the French central bank, which requires them to deposit foreign exchange and other assets in Paris. The CFA offers many economic benefits – primarily stability because it is pegged to the value of the euro – but it is an infantilising hangover from the past that serves as a reminder of African dependency.

For sure, countries that have their own currencies are subject to the destabilising swings of the foreign exchange market, but I believe this also helps foster a sense of accountability. If you announce bad economic policy, your currency plummets and your foreign exchange reserves drain away. These are signals that not even the most powerful despot can ignore.

It was no surprise to me, as I returned to Ivory Coast in 2022, that another phase of decolonisation was underway in French-speaking Africa. By seeking to retain a role for itself, France has made itself a target in African domestic politics. It is wrong to place all of the ills of the current era at its door. And shunning France only to run into the embrace of China or Russia does not represent emancipation or progress. I felt inspired, however, by the desire of the new, young generation of Africans to demonstrate their pride and independence. They have self-esteem in abundance, that most important of qualities. In advancing the cause of their countries, they are building on the work of their elders.

I began thinking about how I could formulate a response to some of these developments – the sliding democratic standards, the discontent – as well as the aspirations and hopes of the next generation on the world's youngest continent. More than a third of the world's young people will live in Africa by 2050, according to the United Nations.[4] During many months of introspection, I asked myself what the value was of my expertise and career unless I applied it in the service of others.

I pondered my tendency to take risks and embrace challenges rather than retreating from them. I could see how all my various roles and passions after Credit Suisse – public service and private sector promotion – could be combined. That's the reason I decided in late 2023 to enter frontline politics and stand for election as the head of my great-uncle Houphouët's party, the PDCI.

It wasn't a decision I took lightly. Entering African politics is not for the faint-hearted. Many people do so for disreputable reasons, seeing it as a path to personal enrichment or a move to escape prosecution. Living in the West, I had everything I needed materially for a comfortable retirement, as well as a host of stimulating positions. But I've never walked away from a challenge – and what could be more rewarding than helping my country and compatriots?

I set about formulating a programme that included the following areas of focus: education, sharing prosperity, upholding the rule of law, embracing new technology, and encouraging sustainable development. But recalling my efforts to make peace and security a focus of Tony Blair's Commission for Africa in 2004, I made this my highest priority.

Ivory Coast has been through a civil war which cut the country in two from 2002 to 2007, followed by a violent post-electoral conflict in 2010–11. Official estimates of the 2010–11 crisis – which nobody believes – are of 3,000 deaths;[5] some human rights organisations have told me privately that they think the real number could be as high as 19,000. Ivorian society has been deeply scarred by these events. In such a highly diverse and fragmented country, there is still a lot of work to be done in order for Ivorians to truly believe in reconciliation.

There is an urgent need to rebuild ties between communities in my country. As a Muslim from a multi-faith family and the head of a political party that is seen as having Christian roots, I hope to be the embodiment of the sort of change I want to see.

I am also a symbol of openness and the product of migration. President Houphouët-Boigny used to say that no country should aspire to be an oasis in the desert. The reason? 'Because it's the desert that wins in the end.' He welcomed migrants from neighbouring countries, even giving them the right to vote in Ivorian elections. Like him, I fundamentally believe that it is Ivory Coast's duty, but also in its interests, to work closely with its neighbours and see them succeed.

I fervently believe democracy is by far the best way of reconciling our country and arbitrating between the competing demands of its communities. But we must be candid in acknowledging that the record of multi-party democracy in much of post-independence Africa is disappointing. To reverse that, we need to rethink and be bold.

President Houphouët-Boigny was not a believer in multi-party democracy as it is practised today. He thought Ivory Coast needed strong, enlightened leadership at independence, that the country was too immature as a state, too riven by divisions, to handle more than one party. In this, he echoed the views of George Washington, American's first and much celebrated president, whose views on political leadership are now mostly forgotten, and were undemocratic by modern standards.

It is worth remembering that African states began their experience with democracy not only woefully underprepared, in terms of institutions and skills, but also with universal suffrage. This is the opposite of what happened in Europe, where the franchise was gradually extended over two centuries, as education and income levels rose. Women only received the vote in many European countries after the Second World War.

Houphouët's record as a sort of enlightened autocrat, during his first twenty years in power, was one of the best in Africa. The introduction of multi-party democracy in 1990 led within less than a decade to what he feared most: the creation of rival parties based on ethnic or tribal identities. Since then, we have had the coup, the civil war, and a string of disputed elections.

One neglected idea that I believe is part of the solution is offering greater representation for minorities. The borders and institutions created for African countries at independence often failed to take into account the diversity of the states they were designed for. Hastily drafted constitutions frequently handed executive powers to a president in a winner-takes-all system. Parliamentary systems or a federal structure that diluted the president's powers might have proved more stable.

The longevity of the United States's constitution, which has endured for nearly 250 years, can be attributed in large part to foresight of the founding fathers who handed states significant autonomy to run their own affairs, while giving them a powerful voice in national politics in the capital. The least populous states, such as Wyoming, get the same number of senators as large ones like California.

This small-state bias can also be seen in the way the president is elected. It is not via the popular vote, but via the electoral college which also dilutes the power of the major population centres. The system is under strain in the era of Donald Trump, but it has helped keep the country peaceful and united, with the notable exception of the 1861–65 Civil War.

The European Union works in a similar way. Each of the twenty-seven nations has a veto over the most sensitive topics of legislation (some decisions can be voted with a qualified majority). This means a small state like Portugal or Lithuania cannot be easily steamrollered by the biggest nations such as France and Germany.

Many African countries would benefit from similar democratic arrangements. Given the way national boundaries were drawn, many nations are fractured along religious lines, such as Ivory Coast with its mostly Muslim north and Christian south. Complex tribal loyalties, as well as ethnic and language differences, add to the rich patchwork of communities.

Clean elections are vital, but it strikes me that many of Africa's democratic problems could also be solved by ensuring that people feel represented by empowered local or regional elected figures. Voters would more easily accept the winner of a contest if they felt it was honest and that their rights as a culture and people would be respected and guaranteed regardless. It is worth remembering that putting an end to Apartheid in South Africa meant offering guarantees to the white minority.

As soon as I took over the PDCI, I began changing the way the party was organised. Decentralisation works in business. I ran both of my businesses as CEO with this as a guiding principle. It works in politics too. We created new representatives at the district level, which were empowered to make their own choices.

For political parties and nations, a strong central authority is still required, of course, in the same way that companies need strong CEOs with vision and authority. Modern African history is full of bloody secessionist movements led by regional political groups looking to break away from the federal state.

But as our democracies mature, entering their seventh decade, perhaps it is time to rethink how power is distributed, to ensure that communities feel better represented. The squabble to claim the all-powerful national executive office, with its privileges and patronage opportunities, is what underpins so much of the political violence and poll-day tension we see today. Constitutional change will be necessary for many countries.

In order to restore faith in African democracy, elected leaders must also demonstrate their ability to generate jobs and opportunities. Quality political leadership allows the private sector to invest and grow, which leads to meaningful economic growth – the sort that brings real improvements in people's lives. I make a distinction here between meaningful economic growth and the sort that is simply measured in GDP statistics. Democratic governments all over the world are grappling with this problem. The growth and jobs statistics leading up to Donald Trump's re-election in November 2024 indicated the American economy was in fine health. But many Americans didn't feel it.

It is the same in Ivory Coast and many other African nations. Ivory Coast has reported strong GDP figures over the last decade under President Alassane Ouattara, but the benefits have not been broad-based. A lot of the growth is the result of population growth, and of extractive industries, which offer few employment opportunities. This can clearly be seen in development statistics. In 1999, when the PDCI government was toppled by the coup, Ivory Coast was ranked 125th in the world Human Development Index (HDI), as calculated every year by the United Nations Development Programme (UNDP). The index measures life expectancy, the number of years spent in education, and purchasing power for 193 countries in the world. By 2010, Ivory Coast had slipped to 172nd.[6]

In 2023, it was ranked 166th but by GDP per capita it was ranked 135th.[7] That difference of forty-one places between our HDI ranking and our relative wealth level is at the heart of the Ivorian tragedy. The economic growth has not been meaningful in terms of improving the quality of life of our citizens.

The Ivorian education system used to be envied across Africa. Many African leaders trained in the country. But sources such as UNESCO and the World Bank suggest that around eight out of ten children under the age of ten are not able to read or write correctly. Final-year secondary school students test at the same level as middle-school children in other countries, when benchmarked internationally. All of this is happening with a school-age population that is growing at around 5 per cent annually.

One of the reasons I became minister of planning and development in 1998 is that the ministry was in charge of demography and population questions, among its many attributions. I have aways believed that demography is destiny for countries. Fluctuations in the birthrate have a huge impact on a country. Demography is the single most important factor determining the future trajectory of countries and societies.

When I started in my job as minister in 1998, I designed and conducted a major demographic study. One of the problems faced by many policymakers in developing countries is the dearth of information on which to base decisions that will have a huge impact on the future of the country. Population data collection is often patchy and other surveys measuring health, income, education, or property are frequently incomplete. It can mean ministers and other decision-makers end up making informed guesses about the way they allocate resources.

As minister, I wanted to know more about the population and, with an eye on the future, how the government needed to prepare for the coming decades. Demography is the one thing that enables you to make predictions with any degree of confidence. It informs you about issues decades in advance, such as how many school places you'll require.

I set about finding skilled demographers who could model the country and project forward to 2015 and beyond. More than a dozen of them took part and I convinced a trio of renowned French experts – Philippe Hugon, Georges Tapinos, and Patrice Vimard – to oversee the work of the collective. Their report for the government, which was published under the title *Ivory Coast at the Dawn of the 21st Century*, was an impressive tome of scholarship.[8] I remember it principally for the warnings it contained: that the country risked major social upheaval and even a coup because of the imbalances in our economy and our uncontrolled population growth.

At more than 500 pages, it was long and dense. It didn't make a public splash and I'm not even sure many people in government or the civil service read it. But I remember talking to President Bédié about the findings, which I found fascinating. I told him about the risk of a coup. His downfall a year later had been foretold.

One of our biggest problems was that we weren't creating enough capacity in the education system. The country's population had quadrupled since independence in 1960, reaching 16 million when I joined the government. Each year, the number of children of school-going age was increasing by 3.8 per cent at the time, one of the highest rates in the world. That meant we needed to increase the number of school places by 3.8 per cent every year, just to stand still. And our ability to open new classrooms was actually gradually falling: only 70 per cent of primary school-age children were being educated in 1995.

Roughly one in every three children was therefore out of school, creating a huge reservoir of unskilled young people, many of whom were destined to become unfulfilled, frustrated and angry about their lack of opportunities. Even those in school faced huge classes of forty or more children, with poor equipment and overstretched teachers – as I had seen during my school years in Abidjan.

Part of the explanation was that the country started behind the curve at its inception. The French colonial authorities built no proper secondary schools, judging education beyond the primary level unnecessary and potentially dangerous for their labouring subjects. There were only a handful of French-trained Ivorian university graduates in the whole nation. At independence, reliable estimates of the school enrolment rate put it at 9 per cent – an appalling number after sixty years of colonisation which ostensibly had the objective of bringing Western, rational education to African populations supposedly beset by ignorance and superstition.

Unsurprisingly given this low starting point, President Houphouët-Boigny, the country's first qualified doctor, made education one of his priorities. Around 40 per cent of the annual budget was dedicated to schooling over the first decades of his rule, a uniquely high proportion of public expenditure by African standards. But when the country ran into financial difficulties in the 1980s and early 1990s, the education budget was one of the victims of the International Monetary Fund-inspired structural adjustment programme.

During this period, interest payments on the national debt rose to 50 per cent of the national budget in some years. In return for emergency financial aid, the IMF demanded stringent cuts in education and health spending. The Washington-based lender of last resort, along with its sister organisation the World Bank, foisted poorly designed and disastrous structural adjustment programmes on Ivory Coast and other developing countries around the world in this era.

Between 1981 and 1994, when I returned to Ivory Coast, not a single new state high school had been built, despite the population surge. The IMF-imposed cuts also meant the government closed many state-funded boarding schools. That might sound a relatively minor loss, but they were used by the children of farmers in remote locations. This meant that the boarding schools were often the only chance for children to gain a secondary education. They were also melting pots, where solid friendships and relationships were built across tribal identities, fostering national unity, and thus playing a huge role in the progress achieved by the country in the 1960s and 1970s.

Borrowing from the IMF and World Bank meant that Ivory Coast was unable to restructure its debts. You can't lengthen the repayment period or lower the interest charges when you're dealing with the IMF or World Bank, as you could with a private lender. Those early-generation structural adjustment programmes effectively ruined the educational prospects of millions of children across the developing world in order to protect the credit ratings and reputations of those lending institutions.

Predictably, poverty, health and educational attainment indicators began reversing. And when you have poverty and low education, you get explosive population growth, which compounds all of your development problems. Once you get trapped in that vicious circle, as so many African states are today, it's incredibly difficult to break out.

If you have explosive population growth coupled with an education system and an economy that cannot provide for the needs of a large part of the population, then you inevitably get political instability. That's part of the explanation for the coup in Ivory Coast in 1999, as well as the rash of putsches which have taken place in recent years. When I returned to my country immediately after the coup, the first mutineering soldier I met told me that he was just eighteen years old: he would have been born in 1981, just as Ivory Coast was entering the acute stage of its debt trap.

I have seen what a difference leadership can make. While I was head of the DCGTx planning agency in the 1990s, we set a target of building 1,700 new classrooms per annum. Along with Prime Minister Duncan at the time, I wasn't doing anything revolutionary. I was just applying basic project management skills, of the sort I later refined and implemented while restructuring Credit Suisse. I was monitoring progress. I targeted waste and delays. I succeeded in motivating people to work hard, to shed their cynicism in pursuit of an essential task for the country.

Education is the one policy area that has the ability to produce positive effects that ripple across all sectors of society and the economy. The demographic study I ordered in 1998, and a host of other academic research, has shown how it is one of the main drivers of lower, sustainable birthrates. The more educated women are, the later they get married; the more likely they are to use contraception, and the fewer children they have. As our study showed, a woman without education had on average 6.2 children, while a woman with a secondary education had 2.3–3.8 children, roughly half the number.

Having fewer children has a host of positive knock-on effects, beyond simply reducing the population pressure on limited resources. The fewer children a family has, the longer the spacing is likely to be between children. That is highly beneficial to the health of the mother and child, by reducing the risk of malnutrition and increasing the resources available to the family.

This is why educating girls has been described as the 'silver bullet' of development policies because it has such powerful multiplier effects. Successful economic development requires a complex package of policies, all delivered at the same time. But educating girls remains one of the single best levers any government can pull.

I have always liked the dictum of sixteenth-century French philosopher Jean Bodin, who stated: 'Il n'y a richesse ni force que d'hommes' – which roughly translates as: 'The only wealth and power is people.' He was making a point that larger populations were beneficial for economic growth, in a book that made a major contribution to the development of demography as an academic subject area. I have a more nuanced view on that point. Writing in 1576, Bodin could not possibly have foreseen the stunning scale of population growth of the late twentieth century and the medical and technological advances which facilitated it. He had no knowledge or concern for the impact of humankind on the climate and global biodiversity.

I agree wholeheartedly, however, that the wealth and power of nations resides in their people, which means that education and health provision are the foundations for national success. You need an educated, healthy, and secure population. All other policy goals are subsidiaries of those three issues.

Take nutrition, for example. We know how important it is as a health and development issue. Malnutrition in pregnant women leads to slower foetal development, stunting and higher child mortality. High child mortality drives up the birthrate because couples have large families in anticipation that some of their offspring will die prematurely. In children under five, poor nutrition also causes slower brain development and cognitive difficulties, greatly reducing their productive capacity as adults.

If you make nutrition – a health issue – your priority, it then drives your agricultural and economic development policies that support farmers. Africa has a major and under-reported problem of crops rotting in the fields, or on the way to markets, or being lost to insects. Some statistics suggest as much as 40 per cent of crops go to waste in these ways. The biggest and most significant impact is on nutrition. If more crops were reaching markets, it would help those areas that currently suffer from chronic shortages and would also lower prices for households everywhere. Families who are now forced to scrimp and save on food, would be able to buy more with the same income.

It's a neglected area of development – and often seen as the domain of the private sector – but retail and distribution are crucial to ensuring crops can be harvested, transported from rural areas and sold to urban consumers for the lowest price possible. As a policymaker, this means you need to focus on providing reliable energy to farmers, giving them access to capital to buy fertilisers and insecticides, and ensuring property rights can be more easily enforced.

It also leads you to identify areas where you most need new infrastructure to bring farm goods to major population centres, with storage facilities and, crucially, refrigeration. Refrigeration requires electricity. So by starting with the vital human issue of health and nutrition, other subsidiary policy priorities – energy, infrastructure, financial services – become evident, all branching off like the roots below the stem.

I'm also incredibly excited by the coming energy revolution, the switch from fossil fuels to renewables. This transition will cause significant upheaval for a handful of major oil producers in Africa, but over the medium term it will help bring low-cost energy to families everywhere and give them access to what are mundane modern-day comforts in the West, such as a refrigerator.

The special purpose acquisition (SPAC) fund I set up after leaving Credit Suisse looked at various possible targets in industries of the future, including in healthcare. But we found it impossible to look past the business opportunities presented by solar energy. The ability of the industry to produce affordable equipment that can deliver low-cost energy is nothing less than extraordinary. The impact has not yet been adequately documented.

The Paris-based International Energy Agency forecasts that solar electricity-generation capacity will surpass that of wind power in 2027 and hydropower in 2029, when it will be the world's biggest renewable energy resource.[9] What these figures don't reveal is where this new energy will have the biggest impact. Because solar does not need electricity grids that are expensive to build and hard to maintain, it will benefit those areas of exponentiality that had previously been without reliable supplies – which includes great swathes of Africa. Solar is relatively quick and easy to install and, once constructed in previously deprived areas, it is transformative in its ability to improve educational, economic, and social outcomes.

My SPAC fund bought out a residential US solar supplier, Complete Solaria, which we then listed on the Nasdaq stock exchange. Complete Solaria is a fully integrated solar producer, meaning it manufactures panels but also offers solar servicing and financing as well. The beauty of the company is its ability to sell high-performing equipment, as well as the financing to clients who might otherwise have hesitated about investing. I hope one day to see the company and others like it play a role in Africa, helping power lighting in schools, refrigeration, computing, and transport for farmers and consumers. Africa is the sunniest continent in the world with the greatest per capita energy needs.

The World Bank runs regular surveys asking businesses in Africa what they need the most. The results are always instructive. The first one is capital, and the second is electricity. We have the tools to be able to solve the energy deficit.

Peace and security, education and health, new technology: these are the building blocks of prosperity in Africa which I hope to focus on as president. Prosperity will be provided through the power and creativity of the business world and entrepreneurs, the fourth pillar of my programme.

I've witnessed the power of the private sector to deliver in Africa when it is unleashed. I was a pioneer when in government in the use of so-called BOOT schemes – build, own, operate, transfer – that saw the Ivorian state partner with companies to deliver infrastructure. This is how we built the hugely successful Foxtrot and Azito power plants in record time. We also devised the Henri Konan Bédié toll bridge in Abidjan, which is privately run and named after my late former political boss. We privatised the airport in the capital, which is still well managed.

Governments often want huge infrastructure projects because the juicy construction contracts offer opportunities for kickbacks and rewarding politically connected allies. Once built, the budgets for maintenance are then siphoned off, meaning within a short period of time the projects fall into disrepair. Most people will shrug, having concluded after decades of mismanagement that this is inevitable, our fate as Africans. However, it doesn't have to be this way. In my view, private ownership leads to superior maintenance, superior performance, and superior user experience. It's about incentives: by transferring ownership to private hands, policymakers create a profit motive. If the operators of a power plant, bridge, airport, or school fail to perform, no one gets paid. They lose money.

Unlike public companies, no one has an incentive to stuff the payroll with acolytes. Corruption and malfeasance hurt their bottom line. Maintenance budgets are sacred because they guarantee the perennity of their operations.

Even when it comes to delivering healthcare, which many Western governments still see as an exclusively state preserve, I have seen the power of private health insurers and providers to improve the lives of people, in countries from Indonesia to India. They also free the government to focus on the neediest.

The future success of Africa will never be decided in international aid organisations or development agencies. It will be decided by entrepreneurs. They are the ones who transformed the lives of Europeans during the industrial revolution, the twentieth-century American boom, and the incredible rise in living standards in East Asia and in China.

I'm regularly invited to economic and business conferences on Africa and am struck by the new generation of entrepreneurs who are brimming with enthusiasm and ambition. They come up to me in the street or at airports. They're confident, creative types, optimistic about technology and how it can transform the lives of their compatriots. They didn't exist in anything like the same numbers ten or twenty years ago. I always tell them that they should be looking to become the stars of African society in the coming decades. In the United States, everyone knows who Bill Gates is, or Elon Musk, but most people don't know the commerce secretary. That is the way things should be. Entrepreneurs are famous because their innovations have transformed their fellow citizens' lives. In francophone Africa, we have inverted it: the route to fame is still seen as being in politics or the civil service.

As well as the new fintech (financial technology) innovators and commercial visionaries, there are hundreds of millions of entrepreneurs all over Africa who are among the hardest working anywhere. Often sole traders supporting a whole family, they run roadside stalls or informal garages, snack bars and dispensaries. Bringing them into the formal economy by offering them financial services would bring an immediate and sustained boost to economies all over Africa. That's why I'm excited when I encounter innovators like Shola Akinlade, a Nigerian who sold his payment company Paystack for $200 million in 2020.

Helping formalise the economy brings a whole host of benefits, rather like educating girls. It has powerful multiplier effects that ripple across the country, opening up new markets, increasing taxation and improving consumer safety. It also helps improve the plight of women who are disproportionately represented in the informal economy with no job or financial security.

I also hope to use my experience in financial services to help Ivory Coast and other African countries run their affairs differently. Although few people seem to share my passion for insurance, I am adamant that the industry is a large missing part of the development puzzle around the world.

We know that the funders of poverty reduction efforts – governments, NGOs, multilateral institutions such as the World Banks – prefer tangible stuff: new roads, new schools, wells. I can see the appeal. They often presume that a combination of aid, loans and more state funding is the magic success formula. More debt is not the solution. Financial services are.

There is a common misconception that banks are one of the most important drivers of growth because they finance the economy through their loans. In Africa, those loans are often prohibitively expensive, meaning entrepreneurs must look elsewhere, to family and friends, for money to start or grow their businesses.

What really supercharges an economy is equity – equity capital which is invested in companies. And life-insurance companies and pension funds are usually the main providers of equity capital. They own the largest pools of capital that can be invested long-term to fuel the productive parts of the economy. For example, New York-based BlackRock, the world's biggest investor, doesn't own the funds it places in companies around the world. It is investing the savings of millions of American teachers, office workers, or small business owners who are putting aside money for a rainy day or retirement or to protect their loved ones.

Prudential started in 1848 and was one of the first investors in the London Stock Exchange. The funds were made up of small contributions from investors who wanted to put their savings to work. The company remains one of the biggest investors in listed British companies.

Africa desperately needs such institutional investors, who would put money into African companies. When run correctly, insurance companies are vital to the sort of development I want to see: job-creating, opportunity-providing, wealth-producing economic growth.

I have spent part of my last few years advising governments in Africa. I find them generally focused on public sector investment. I tell them one of the biggest changes they could bring about is helping facilitate life-insurance providers, private pension funds, and other asset managers. Africa does not lack entrepreneurs. It is teeming with them. What we lack are the sorts of medium- and large-sized companies, particularly in the manufacturing sector, which need capital investment.

When I was CEO of Prudential I oversaw the expansion of Prudential into Africa. I set up a committee with a mandate to look for opportunities on the continent. They reported back to the board what I knew already: that there were few competitors and an emerging class of savers who wanted to invest their money. We bought our first African life-insurance businesses in Ghana and Kenya in 2014, the year before I left. The current Prudential CEO, Anil Wadhwani, also believes the continent is in the early stages of the growth path taken by East Asian markets.

The other idea I frequently pitch to African governments, and hope to implement in Ivory Coast, is the creation of sovereign wealth funds. It's an idea that I have been keen on since the 1980s, when I respectfully but forcefully disagreed with one of President Houphouët's boldest economic policies. Upset by falls in the price of cacao, and outraged that Western companies made such huge profits from making chocolate, Houphouët ordered an embargo on cacao exports in 1988 in a bid to drive the price higher. Although I sympathised with the objective and was troubled, like him, by the plight of Ivorian planters, I had major misgivings. I feared that Ivory Coast would be unable to move the market on its own despite the country's large market share in global cacao supplies. We were facing new competition from countries such as Malaysia and Indonesia, which could be tapped for alternative supplies. Another problem was that cacao is perishable by nature. It can only be stocked for so long – meaning buyers knew they could wait Houphouët out.

In the end, huge stocks of Ivorian cacao built up, rotted, and became valueless. The international price barely moved and Houphouët felt betrayed to the end of his life, convinced that Western buyers and market speculators had combined to fleece Ivorian growers who toiled in the fields each day.

Despite the huge cost to the country, many Ivorians applauded an attempt to correct an injustice: that those doing the cutting and carrying on plantations, those caring for the cacao trees, took such a small share of the final price of a chocolate bar. The same imbalance exists in the coffee industry, where the raw material is sold cheaply by the tonne before being converted into £5 drinks in Western cities.

My argument was that we couldn't change the global value chain, which transported agricultural products from the jungle onto ships, into plants, into packaging factories and then finally into consumers' mouths via a supermarket, shop, café or bistro. Each step adds value, with the final stage – the coffee shop or retailer – often adding the most. Without that chain, the coffee is nearly worthless.

Clearly, there are inequalities: the power of multinational buyers gives them often unfair advantages of scale. It needs to be countered by some form of collective bargaining from the sellers. But my argument to President Houphouët was that instead of taking on multinationals and the markets, he should try to play their game. Why not buy shares in Nestlé or Kraft or Mars, Starbucks or Coca-Cola? Their shares are able to deliver a dividend every year for eternity. Then you have a cut of the final chocolate and coffee price. If Ivory Coast had invested part of its windfall from the 1970s food commodities boom, we'd be sat today on huge gains.

The Gulf countries began investing their oil income half a century ago and have accelerated their efforts over the last two decades. They can see the end of their fossil fuel bonanza and are preparing for the future by diversifying. Saudi Arabia's Public Investment Fund – the country's sovereign wealth fund – has assets of around $700 billion under management, while the Abu Dhabi Investment Authority (ADIA) is estimated to oversee nearly $1 trillion.

Rents need to be invested, not consumed. One needs only to look where the Gulf nations are today, with their wealth per capita and development indicators, compared with oil-rich African states, to see the impact of superior governance and a different long-term private investment approach. They serve as an example for African countries.

Owning shares would also give commodity-producing African countries a voice and ear inside the companies whose decisions affect them significantly – from the creation or closure of processing plants to new supply decisions. The Democratic Republic of Congo, one of the most resource-rich countries in the world, should, for instance, own shares in Glencore, the world's biggest raw material trading company. Anglo-Swiss multinational Glencore is one of the biggest miners of Congolese cobalt and copper.

Getting a greater share of the overall value chain located on African soil is the next step in the continent's development. More and more of the basic transformation of commodities is being shifted to producer countries, away from developed ones. Reliable energy, good infrastructure, political stability, and the rule of law are vital in encouraging this process. In the meantime, nothing stops states taking stakes in the companies that profit the most from their labour or resources.

All the issues I've highlighted in this final chapter – security, democracy, health and education, new technology, and economic growth – form the core of my programme for Ivorians. My other priority is pursuing sustainable development, ensuring Ivory Coast and Africa more broadly is preserved for future generations.

I firmly believe that the twenty-first century can be Africa's century if policymakers deliver the right raft of policies to take advantage of the incredible natural gifts bestowed on the continent and the creativity and energy of its people. Voters are crying out for these basic building blocks of well-being and prosperity. They are desperate for clean and effective public administration.

When I used to talk about the potential of Africa, some people used to dismiss me.

'If you take all of sub-Saharan Africa's GDP, it's about the same size as Belgium's,'* was a line repeated throughout the 1980s, at every conference on Africa. The point today is that Africa's GDP stands at $3.2 trillion, about the same as India's with a similar population. Belgium's is still at about $800 billion.

Perhaps because of my background in Ivory Coast, as a CEO I always looked for exponential growth. I wanted markets that grow as nature grows, with the number of cells and sophistication multiplying over time, a process that in Homo sapiens starts with an embryo and ends as a human being. It's different to linear

---

* At around $700–800 billion.

growth, which is steady and constant. All of nature functions exponentially.

I think the idea of exponentiality is easier to grasp as someone from the emerging world. In our lifetimes, we've seen the impact of exponential growth on our lives: on our populations and cities; on the number of surfaced roads; on university graduates. All have grown exponentially, like the global sales of Amazon or Apple.

Europeans tend to think in terms of linear growth, incremental change over years, because that is the visible pace of most things on the continent. Economies plod along with 2 or 3 per cent growth in a boom year. But the industrial revolution and European colonial empires were not built linearly. They were exponential. I suspect Europeans understood exponentiality more clearly in the eighteenth and nineteenth centuries.

Americans on the other hand have an innate appreciation of exponentiality. In so many ways, from their business culture to the way wealth is distributed within their society, Americans are a combination of emerging markets and the older countries. That's what makes them such redoubtable business people.

In both my CEO jobs, I looked to position both companies to harness the exponential growth that was taking place in East Asia. That region has been the engine of the global economy and wealth creation for the last three decades.

I'm convinced that many African countries are in the same position as their East Asian peers in the 1970s and 1980s. Africa now needs responsible, forward-looking leadership that puts the interests of the collective first, as Deng Xiaoping did in China or Lee Kuan Yew did in Singapore.

We could have decades of high growth ahead of us. Our demography is a challenge, but also represents a huge opportunity. At a time when much of the Western world and China are ageing, Africa's youth and vigour can be a comparative advantage, if young people are given the education and work opportunities that they crave and deserve.

Our continent has everything it needs to succeed, enabling it to write a different narrative for itself from the colonial and post-colonial periods, dominated as they are by social upheaval, exploitation, and poverty. The final mental chains of slavery – the lack of confidence, the tendency to seek approval or praise from others – are being smashed by the new generations. All of this, God willing, is set to be the focus of the final stage of my working life, back home where I belong.

NOTES

Chapter 5

1. <<tk, newspaper article citations for 'created history', and 'first black boss' refs>>.
2. https://www.thetimes.com/sunday-times-100-fast-growth/company-profile/article/profile-tidjane-thiam-exotic-past-of-the-man-from-the-pru-xql6sr80rgl?region=global
3. <<tk, FT/'shambles'>>.
4. <<tk, Telegraph/ 'incompetent fool'>>
5. <<tk? one senior investor>>.
6. <<tk, The Times/Ibiza>>.

Chapter 6

1. https://www.euromoney.com/article/27bjsstsqxhkmh1v3mehh/awards/banker-of-the-year-2018-tidjane-thiam-credit-suisse
2. <<tk, FT/'saw race everywhere'>>
3. Duncan Mavin, *Meltdown: Scandal, Sleaze and the Collapse of Credit Suisse* <<pub details – i.e. location and year>>, <<p.?>>.

Chapter 7

1. https://www.afrobarometer.org/feature/flagship-report/
2. https://www.afrobarometer.org/feature/flagship-report/
3. https://www.uky.edu/~clthyn2/coup_data/home.htm

4. *UN World Population Prospects 2022* (https://www.un.org/development/desa/pd/sites/www.un.org.development.desa.pd/files/wpp2022_summary_of_results.pdf).

5. https://www.reuters.com/article/world/hundreds-executed-by-both-sides-in-ivorian-war-report-idUSBRE8790WE/

6. https://hdr.undp.org/content/human-development-report-2023-24

7. <<endnote tk>>.

8. https://horizon.documentation.ird.fr/exl-doc/pleins_textes/divers17-09/010030174.pdf

9. https://www.iea.org/reports/renewables-2024/global-overview

INDEX